Without Consent

Sid Spencer

"Healing doesn't mean the damage never existed.

It means the damage no long controls our life"

Anon

My Endless Thanks go to:

My amazing, funny, loving husband, Kevin. I thank you for all the strength that you give me.

The laughter that we share and the forgiveness you grace me with.

Thank you for telling me I matter and helping me to heal.

To the following Charities, Survivors UK, Life Centre Worthing and Mankind UK in Brighton.

The patience, kindness and time to breathe that you have given me have been life-saving.

Further thanks go to my sister Julie and to my good friends Debbie and Princess for being there when I needed to talk.

To Becky, Louise, Lesley, and Michelle, for reading my words and giving me valuable feedback.

To Brian, all the way up in Scotland, a man that genuinely understands but doesn't quite realise his own strength.

To my friend and neighbour Liz for all our hugs on those difficult days.

To Sussex Police for believing me, for helping me to right the wrongs and the guidance they provided throughout.

To Katy and Bradley, our two amazing kids, for showing me how important it is for all children to heal and be listened to and for helping the child that I was, to laugh out loud again.

And finally, to that very boy that I was, that I still am and that I am so proud of,

Thank you for your incredible strength, for holding on, and for always keeping the essence of who I indeed was, safely buried inside me.

PROLOGUE

This is my story; it's about my life and what I experienced as a child growing up in the care system. It is a real account; these are my memories.

Some names have been changed, not to protect the guilty but to protect their families.

It's a memoir that covers a dark part of my childhood, but it is also about hope, strength, and justice and I hope that becomes obvious as you read on.

I like to think of myself as a good person, a person that genuinely cares about those that I know and the world that we live in.

I am flawed, I live with crippling anxiety, with a depression that is always there but some days are better than others, although that damn black dog still bites hard at times.

There are periods when I can have very little self-worth, although, as I said, I think I am a good person.

I have hurt people in my life, and for that, I am incredibly sorry, I have judged, and I have regretted it. I have stopped good people from getting close, and I have allowed the wrong types to get closer.

I struggle with my weight because of years of comfort eating, and I no longer have issues with alcohol and drugs because they controlled me too much in my 20's, a key through a doorway into a world that was numb from emotion and fear.

I have made mistakes, some foolish mistakes.

I tend to fare better when I am alone as people worry me, because of my past I have a suspicion which I try to overcome. I find making friendships very difficult.

I get frustrated when I am not listened to, and I get hurt when others don't try to understand me.

That isn't about me needing to be right; it is just solely about being listened to, another consequence of my childhood.

Honesty is essential to me, and I am a sincere person myself.

I tend only to feel safe when I am with my husband or at home, which can make life difficult. I adore my kids, and I would die for them. I try to give them the childhood that I was robbed off.

I don't feel sorry for myself although I can feel very alone. I wish I could welcome more people into my life but, to be honest, I just can't.

I am a fighter, I am strong, and I am direct. I love music, reading, and my little family; I am fun, kind-hearted and genuine. I am surprised that I am here today. I am amazed that I have the life I do.

I, like so many others in this world, didn't have the best start in life.

This is my story, my journey and what you will read is an honest account of my life as a child in the care system in the 1970's & 1980's.

I believe that although it has been one hell of a trip to get where I am today, the strength I have inside me becomes obvious to see throughout this book.

CHAPTER ONE

The internet these days seems to be full of inspirational quotes about moving on, letting go of your past, not letting it affect your present and so on. But the fact is that we are all affected by them, all events are character building, and they all leave an imprint on our very beings, either enriching our souls or leaving yet another scar from a battle survived.

Social media sites are full of quotes about this very topic, people post them in their thousands, and usually, they are written with an artistic font and placed over beautiful pictures of fields, oceans, puppies or people hugging one another.

I'm not against these quotes. In fact, some of them are very sweet, with a truthful, thought-provoking twist that can make you feel good. They can reign in your thoughts and remind you of a promise you made to yourself, or at least give you a spiritual kick up the backside, I've even been guilty of posting a few myself.

What confuses and at times concerns me is that if you have grown up in a safe and secure family; if you had people consistently trying their best for you, even if it didn't feel like it at the time you were growing up. If people have cared and nurtured your talents and allowed and encouraged you to explore the best that you could be, then surely no one would tell you to leave your past behind you? You wouldn't hear anyone same "move on, don't let that experience influence the person you will become."

If you have survived a life-threatening illness or accident, overcome adversity or even if you have won the lottery, then these events would have played a significant part in who you have become. People will expect and encourage you to embrace it, to remember what you have achieved from those times and the battles you have won. So why is it that if you have been a child who was abused or neglected in the care system, or if you were attacked or raped and later in life, you have found the strength to talk about it or face your abuser or attacker, why do so many people react so negatively towards you? Judge you, and go silent? Why do so many people say that you need to let go of it? Move on? Don't let it affect your life now, and stop being a victim?

Everything that happens to us, whether that be positive or negative, makes us who we are today. How we choose to use those experiences and the knowledge they provide is where it becomes complicated.

You might be appalled at the very thought of someone judging a survivor of rape or abuse, but it happens. You might vehemently disagree with me and it might be a confusing statement to read or accept, but it is a fact. How do I know it's a fact? Because I have lived it, because

I am a survivor of abuse and rape and because I have had my character judged, people have reacted strangely, at times in a hostile manner towards me, and many have called me a liar.

People find it hard to talk about child rape and abuse, it is a terrible, dreadful thing, it is simply pure evil and violent and destroys so much in the victim.

There appears to be fear from others about listening to victims and survivors, and perhaps that's one of the reasons that it goes unnoticed for so long. Why people suffer in silence and these sick people thrive. It used to be the same with domestic violence, so many people living in silence and fear but now we know, as a society, that it's entirely unacceptable and people speak out, and more importantly people are listening. That is where we need to get to with child abuse and rape as well, and we need to get there now!

....

In the last few years, the stories of the rape and abuse by various celebrities have shocked the country.

So many people have reacted in a way that I have personally found very distasteful.

Jokes about child sexual abuse have been shared, posted on social media sites and also said at live comedy shows.

How anyone in their right mind can find a joke about a child being abused amusing, is entirely beyond me.

Taking an accused celebrities unique selling point and turning it into a joke about them abusing children or vulnerable adults is not something that I can comprehend. Using a funny rhyme to twist a tale about someone being hurt is something that I have never found comfortable, but it sadly happens so much.

I find it a real worry when someone can joke about cruelty on any level, and personally I have ended friendships over this.

Growing up in the care system in the 1970's and 1980's was not a good time for me. There was little concern with what I needed, no interest in my development and wishes, and there indeed wasn't any urgency in giving me a voice.

This book isn't about me going on and on about how terrible my childhood was, how no one cared and how it had a prolonged and adverse effect on most of my life, although I will be discussing that a lot.

What I hope you will get from this is a sense of my strength, a strength that doesn't just live within me but is there for us all, a strength that unites others, that conquers the dark.

It is about the truth, about what happened to me and thousands of other children in care. It is about how the 'system' failed and how it is still failing today on many levels. It's about my experience of coming out the other side, of becoming a foster carer with my husband and then adopting our two amazing kids, creating the family life and security for them that I never had. It is about survival, taking control, holding people and local authorities to account for what they did and didn't do and hopefully, it's about waking up the belief in other people that they can do everything that I have done. It's about getting others to see that what happened to them wasn't OK, that they do have a voice, however many years ago that the terrible event occurred, and that people will listen, will believe and do care.

CHAPTER TWO

My mother and father should never have been parents, and they lacked any compassion or love for anyone else other than themselves. A product of their own chaotic upbringings, their dysfunctional birth families, had shifted all their inherited issues on to them, resulting in my parents being doomed before they had even met.

My father was a handsome rogue that was adored by all the girls, and a few boys too as the story goes. With his long legs and his thick dark hair which was always in a quiff of sorts and his cheeky crooked smile, he was fondly nicknamed "Spidey," and his narcissistic personality captivated people and ultimately caused most of them a lot of heartache. In his life to date, he has had three marriages, which I know of, and no doubt countless children. My sister and I were the first, we know of our half-sister, and there is a younger half-brother, who I have never met. I dread to think how many more there are.

My Dad is a user, a chancer, and a heartbreaker. Selfish to the core, he only latches on to people when they are of a benefit to him. He has worked as a fishmonger, a milkman, a fish and chip shop owner, a pub landlord, a lorry driver and a taxi driver, and he has also served time at her Majesty's pleasure, more than once. His current whereabouts are not known. It is believed that he is still in Brighton.

My mother was petite, blonde, beautiful and ample breasted. Like my father she too had a very narcissistic personality and was a huge flirt. She always needed reassurance that she was lovable and beautiful, and when my father stopped fulfilling this role she soon realised that Vodka could equally make her feel amazing. Unfortunately for my sister and I, the Vodka had another spell at the bottom of its many bottles, and that was to make her forget she had two young kids that needed her. Mum only had two children, Julie, my older sister and me. I believe she has experienced numerous miscarriages, which I can't help but think now were blessings in disguise.

After heading to Bournemouth in the late 1970's after hearing that my dad had moved there, she eventually remarried to someone else when it turned out not to be true. She entered into another unhealthy marriage that was also rife with adultery on both sides, plenty of alcohol and violence.

There has been one consistent friend to my mum throughout her life, and that is the drink. It has comforted her, it has teased her, it has whispered in her ears, and it has always won.

As I write this, Mum is currently in a nursing home back in Brighton, just a few roads from where her life with my father began decades ago, she has Korsakoff Syndrome, an alcohol-related form of Alzheimer's.

She doesn't know who anyone is anymore, she is unable to walk or feed herself, and she is only 68 years old. My mum is now a shell of a woman and although entirely too late, my mum is now dry.

It is sad to see my mum like this. She was a fun, bright, beautiful woman, not a great mum, but for a while, after I contacted her when I was 19 years old, we shared some great times together, and I grew to love her. She never got to be the mum she would have enjoyed being, always too weak to look after anyone, even herself.

……………………………………………..

Both my parents liked to party in the 1970's, which for them meant lots of drinking and smoking pot; they were a fashionable, attractive young couple and therefore very popular, a fact that they both thrived on.

Years later my mother told me of the swingers' parties they would attend, the group sex and the jealousy and paranoia that their behaviour bred. Her drinking increased and not just socially. My mother has always been a very emotional being, and the secret alcohol mixed with the tonic of mistrust soon started to destroy her marriage and our family home.

My father also had an addiction all of his own, he was addicted to sex, and he screwed around a lot, whoever and whenever he could, and apparently this is still his favourite past time.

For a period in 1974/75, my parents had two fish and chip shops in Croydon, South London. We lived above one in New Addington which was run mainly by our mother, and which we lived above. My father concentrated on another at the other end of town. He only employed beautiful young women in his shops, and this must have driven my mother mad. Plagued by her demons and suspicions, she had no control over what her charmer of a husband was doing over at the other end of town.

I remember the fights in the evenings at home. Dad, coming home to my mum's rage after she had been stewing for 7 or 8 hours in her jealousy and alcohol. Her fears were taunting her, playing with her mind and telling her what she knew in her heart was right. In the days of no internet or mobile phones, it must have been tough on her, with no way of being able to check up on him. It really isn't a surprise that she would seek comfort from the bottom of a bottle.

But then one day my mum decided enough was enough, and that it was time to visit my dad as he worked hard in their other shop at the other end of Croydon.

The story goes that when she arrived there at midday, while my sister and I were at school, the shop was closed. Not having any keys, she peered through the large window to seek out life, but no sign of fish and chips being fried could be seen. Remembering that there was a back door to the shop through a yard at the rear, she set off to enter secretly. The back door was open, and his jet-black Capri was parked by the waste bins. My mum headed to the potato peeling room, which was usually stacked high with brown paper sacks of spuds, a sink, and a giant dominating peeling machine.

But what met my poor mums' eyes that day couldn't have been a very welcoming sight for her.

There, sprawled on her back, over a lumpy sack of Maris pipers with my father between her legs, was the sweet 18-year-old shop assistant that had recently been employed by him. My poor Mum, what a dreadful thing to walk into and witness.

When they fought it was deafening, my sister and I would sit at the top of the stairs and listen to our Mum scream. I don't have any memories of Dad raising his voice, but he must have, what I do remember though was that the screaming would stop after a sharp smack sound from my

Dad striking her across the face. Domestic violence, as it would be recognised to be now, was rife in our family.

Smashed bottles, slammed doors and air born ashtrays were not a rare sight in our home. In the mornings I would often creep out on the landing to judge what the atmosphere might be and would usually just hear the slamming of the front door, dad heading off to the peeling room across town as mum laid in bed, or on the sofa in the messed-up lounge.

Mum never hit me, or at least I have no memories of it, but I do remember her attacking my sister.

Smacks across my sister's face and the pulling of her hair were a regular thing in New Addington.

One morning before school, she hit my sister with such force in the bathroom as she ran a hot bath for herself that my poor sister ended up immersed in the water while wearing her school uniform. On another morning, again before school, Mum was screaming at my sister in the Fish and Chip shop downstairs, and somehow the belt of my sisters' coat ended up in the chip fryer, because of Mum again lashing out at her.

It's easy to see these days why my sister took the brunt of mums drunken, hungover, and jealous fuelled anger. My dad was flirting with other women, he was shagging behind her back and indeed, also in front of her at their swingers' parties, and clearly, this ate away at her. She screamed at him, cried and begged him to stop, but he didn't so, she turned it on my sister, another female who took the attention of my dad away from her, and she did not like it. Mum treated me with indifference, and I wasn't important to her, she was often not aware of my whereabouts, I could often be found three doors up at a friend's flat, having walked out of our chaotic home by myself, at just five years old.

It's strange, or maybe not, but when I spoke to my sister about this 30 plus years later she had no memory of it happening to her, she readily admitted to blocking a lot of stuff out.

During this turbulent, violent period, we moved back to our hometown, Brighton, probably an attempt by Mum to remove Dad from his girlfriend and to be close to her family again, but it wasn't long after that, that their marriage was over. I remember an occasion when mum had forgotten to collect her 6-year-old son from school because she was too stoned on marijuana. I remember the final night we were all to stay at the one-bedroom basement flat in Queens Park. I remember the worse fight I had ever seen between them, with dad slapping and kicking mum in the front room, who was again, drunk.

I remember mum running out of the flat into the night, screaming and crying and disappearing into the dark. Dad was then getting my sister and me into his car as he then drove frantically around the streets of Brighton as we looked for her out of the back windows. I remember my sister seeing mum crouching outside the flat by the bay windows and dad then dragging her up the concrete steps and throwing her into the passenger seat. The screaming, the tears, my sister and I in the back, terrified, grabbing and hitting mum and dad's shoulders, pleading for them to stop, dad shouting at all of us to shut up.

I remember my mum reached over to my dad and scratched his face. With so much force I thought mum would get pushed out of the car, dad pushed her off, sending the left side of her face crashing into the door window. Now, as an adult, I see that what we were witnessing was domestic violence and I think that that did carry on into future relationships with both my sister and me.

My next memory of that night is that we were all back in the flat. Mum and dad are now sat together on their double bed, and my sister and I are on the top bunk of our bunk beds in the left corner of the room, they are both calmer now, although mums face is red raw, and a considerable bruise is developing on the left side.

They told us they were splitting up for good, and then strangely asked us who we wanted to live with.

My sister was quick off the mark and said dad and I chose mum. I don't have any memory of us all then going our separate ways, what I remember next is us all being at the social services office down near the Old Steine area, I remember mum and dad going into a room with a social worker while we waited in the white waiting area. My final memory of that day was mum and dad explaining they were going but we were to stay with the social worker who was going to find us somewhere to stay.

During the fighting, all the alcohol, and the collapse of my family, I suffered from horrendous nightmares. I would dream that the air around me was heavy, weighing me down and stretching my limbs. I would wake up in pain, the bones in my legs and arms aching. My throat was always so tight after these dreams and swallowing was always difficult, it was as if I had been strangled. I used to get up and run around the sofa in the lounge; I remember Mum asking me what I was doing once, and I told her that the running stopped the air from squeezing me as it couldn't catch me. It is evident to me today that these were my early introduction to the anxiety attacks that have plagued my life since.

Once we had been taken in to care, and my parents had gone their separate ways, my nightmares and the imposing compressing air stopped.

Over the eight years that we were a family my Mum had stabbed herself, cut her wrists twice, taken an overdose three times and been beaten up numerous times by her husband. That was not the ideal setting for two small children.

……………………………………………..

1976

Our first foster family, and to be my sister's only, was with an experienced couple who had already opened their home and family to so many other children for many years before.

I remember being so nervous and excited when our social worker took us there, that within minutes of walking into the hallway of the large house I had knocked over and smashed an ornament.

I was six years old, and my sister was eight, and a whole new chapter of childhood was just opening up for us.

The house was a five floored Edwardian townhouse, and for us, two kids that had just come from a one bedroomed flat with an outdoor loo, it was mind-blowing. Our new family was Bi-European, our foster mother was English, but the new father figure in our life was from Germany, which seemed very exotic to us.

The family was run with an iron fist, there were house rules for just about everything, and it soon became apparent to us that there was an unspoken understanding between all the adults living in this grand house. These two new kids were purely there for two reasons only, one, for the money that was paid by the local authority and secondly, to clean, wash up, walk the dogs and run around after everyone else.

I have no memories of being hugged by my replacement mum, and there were indeed no declarations of love or of them being proud of us. We were never made to feel wanted. The only physical contact was when we were being slapped for not doing something to their standard or punished for being naughty. Our past wasn't spoken about, and there wasn't any therapeutic care in those days at all. Both my sister and I have clear memories of being made to sit at the table and eat all of the food that had been placed in front of us. Threats of a clip around the ear, and announcements of how the world was full of many more grateful kids than us, would only make us resist eating the food even more. To this day the memory of chewing on hard, cold, curled up liver still turns our stomachs.

Our foster dad hardly ever spoke or acknowledged us. He always seemed to be sitting in his chair in the adult lounge, smoking his roll-ups, watching the horse racing or listening to the music that reminded him of his battles in World War Two. The room was often filled with the tunes of Gracie Fields singing 'Wish me luck' or the Beverly Sister's asking him not to sit underneath the apple tree without them. The air mixed with their sweet voices and the smell of his Old Holburn tobacco and it intrigued me, as we were rarely allowed to enter. I was afraid of him during my time there; he scared me with his disinterest in what was going on around him, he reminded me of a ghost, an entity drifting in a different world from the rest of us that would occasionally cross over to ours. The coughing and wheezing from his damaged lungs, which he inherited from his time as a POW during the Second World War, always announced that he was somewhere nearby.

In later years, I realised that he was probably battling his own demons. The horrific, internal scarring from the memories of his time in a prisoner of war camp, the possible shame of what Hitler did under the name of his home country, the loss of his family and the knowledge of his wife's ongoing affair under his very own roof with their long-standing 'lodger.' The lounge, his chair, his music and his smokes were his sanctuary away from the chaotic atmosphere of his home and the many kids from other families that had invaded it over the years.

I have often wondered if he too was ruled by the very same iron fist that dictated our lives in that cold, unwelcoming Edwardian house. It was the late 1970's and Margaret Thatcher wasn't the only Iron Lady that was controlling the lives of others.

My time with our new family was cut short one day when I returned home from school to find my social worker waiting for me, and a small suitcase sat in the hallway. It was explained to me that it had been decided that I was leaving because of my recent bad behaviour, I had been caught trying to take a small leather-bound radio, belonging to my foster mums' lover, to school that morning. I was told they were now looking for a younger family for me, but that Julie, my sister, would be staying where she was. My soon to be ex-foster mum knelt to face me and told me that this was not what she wanted. She went on to explain that it was the decision of the social services, as they felt I needed a younger family and at that moment, for the first time, I felt that this stern woman really did care about me, as she clasped me to her bosom and I breathed in her sweet perfume.

In 1990, as a young adult desperate for answers about my childhood, I had requested to see the records of my time in care. It was arranged for me to visit an office and with someone present, I would be able to go through them and take notes. I remember feeling sick with anxiety that day, and I was worried about what I might find out but equally excited that finally, I would get a better understanding of why my time in care had been so fragmented and damaging. The notes about my birth parents were pretty much what I expected and remembered, drunken fights, poor parenting, and dads many affairs. When I got to read about my time at my first foster family, the lack of compassion and love was clear to see, the review notes were to the point, and there were little praise and nothing that I read surprised me until I read about that day when I was to leave them.

In front of me, in clear typed font, the page told me that it was at the request of my foster mum that I am removed from the family immediately. The reason given was due to my continuous lousy behaviour at home and school and the fighting with my sister and their adopted daughter. I sat there numb with shock. This wasn't what she had told me, and my memory was clear about her saying she didn't want me to leave. I could see her face close to mine as she knelt, I heard her words about the social worker wanting me to have a younger family, I remembered her sweet perfume. I felt the emotion inside me again from that day and the fear of leaving rose inside. There in black and white was the truth; it was her that wanted me gone. The words on the ageing page went on to inform me, that extra support had been offered to help her with my apparent terrible behaviour, but it had been declined.

In one swift turn of a page, a memory that I had held for years, a memory that had told me an adult had cared about me, was destroyed. A memory that I had often revisited over the years of abuse and neglect that followed, that had been a source of comfort to me, had been revealed to be a lie. After leaving their family and my sister, I did, for the next 14 years or so, keep in touch with them all. The knowledge that it wasn't them that didn't want me, that it was the social services fault, was a comfort to me but now, at that moment, sat in that office with that stranger, I learned the cold truth. It was a lie, and it was a lie that this woman carried on telling me through all the years leading up to that point in time.

My heart was broken. I sat there, and I cried, my body shook from the sobbing, the realisation that this foster family and the two that followed them had never truly loved me, the awareness that all the adults in my childhood had let me down, starting with my birth parents, ripped through my soul.

The truth that the one memory I had, that involved an adult in a parental role that had often been used as a source of comfort had been destroyed, and it made me break down.

Back in 1978, after saying goodbye to my sister, I found myself sitting on a bed in a large dormitory of a children's home at the other end of town feeling absolutely petrified, the room was huge with five beds down each side and four wardrobes for clothes. The wallpaper was a dark mustard colour, which did nothing but make the room feel even more imposing. At the end of the room was a large sash window, the white paint on the wood was falling off, no doubt helped by little fingers picking away at it, the curtain was a dark navy blue and had a couple of torn flaps in it, two of the square window panes were cracked.

The sounds of kids that I didn't know buzzing and enquiring about me in the hallway outside the room, added to my fear; my legs shook as they dangled over the edge of the bed, not quite reaching the threadbare carpet. The sensation of hot urine filled my trousers as I lost control of myself and I quickly jumped up, hoping it hadn't seeped through to my new bed. This was not the day that I had expected when I left for school that morning.

Looking back now, and as a parent to two kids from very similar backgrounds, it is indeed incredible, and not in a good way, that an adult would get rid of a child in their care because of bad behaviour.

I wasn't violent or threatening. I wasn't hurting people or even being verbally abusive. I was shoplifting sweets with my mates from school, taking things from home to show off, and I had some sibling rivalry with my sister. Yes, I fought with my sister, but we never put each other in a hospital!

All these things could have been sorted out with firm boundaries. What is even more incredible is that this was an experienced foster carer who had been fostering children for decades, and had five kids of their own, and grandchildren. Again, for the boy I was, it was just another confirmation that I was not loved or loveable.

The children's home was still in Brighton, so I could go to the same primary school, Stanford Middle, a sizeable Victorian school that overlooked Brighton's railway lines.

I was able to still be with my friends who gave me great comfort, and one of my mates only lived a road away from where I was now going to be living.

Although I saw my sister at school every day, we didn't hang around with each other. This was normal for us and had been that way when we were both with the same foster family, we had our circle of friends, and with my sister fast approaching being a teenager, it was not cool for her to be seen with her little brother.

CHAPTER THREE

Saint Anne's Home for Children was a huge home that was run by a Catholic order of Nuns, The Poor Servants of The Mother of God. The Order was founded in 1872 by Mother Magdalen Taylor to undertake social care work within the community, and the nuns moved to Hove in 1948 from their Brighton premises after severe damage in World War Two. It was just around the corner from the beautiful St Anne's Well Garden, one of the towns beautiful parks. I was pleased as it was now the route I would take to school every morning. I would save up the crusts and burnt toast from the homes manic communal kitchen each morning and leave a little earlier than most of the other kids, so I could feed the squirrels in the park.

It's funny, because now as an adult when I'm with people, and they are sharing stories of their happy childhood memories, I realise that none of mine include any people.

My happiest boarding school memories are when I am alone, sitting amongst the bushes in the local park feeding the squirrels. I remember that after they had gotten used to me, they would come and take the food from my hand.

Also, once, while sat in the bluebell woods with my sketch pad, drawings trees, I became aware of four badger cubs that had come out of their den to see what I was doing. I sat so still that they rolled around on my jacket which was lying next to me. Another fond memory is of me sitting on a fallen tree trunk that went out over a lake, fishing, relaxing quietly alone when a Heron flew down and sat next to me. But by far, one of my favourite times was in the hot weather when I would sprawl on top of the Pigsty roof with a large watering can, showering the Gloucestershire Old Spot pig as she danced around in the shower.

All of these were such magical moments in my life.

……………………………………………..

The children's home was mixed with boys and girls, and it was separated into 'houses' within the vast building.

With its own playground area and grassed lawns and a separate Holy wing for the Nuns and Sister Superior, it was a magnificent building. There were also two different houses within the grounds that housed Vietnamese refugees, and all us kids use to go over there whenever we could and play with the small children, as well as eat some fantastic food.

Once I had gotten over the fear of not being in a family unit I was delighted to be there. The Nuns ruled the houses, and there were staff too, my time there was very happy, and I can honestly say that if I had been left to spend the rest of my childhood there, then it probably would have been a more positive way for a child to live.

We enjoyed days out, holidays to Butlin's, where I won a ballroom dancing competition at the age of 9 with the lovely Sister Cathy, one of the youngest nuns at the home. She was fun to be around and so gentle and loving, I felt safe with these people, and I felt loved.

My social worker continued to visit me, informing me each time that the search was on to find me a new family. My pleas to stay at Saint Anne's were always ignored.

Then, a couple of months later I was told that a new family had been found, and my stomach did a flip from the anxiety of having to start another new life.

....

There were no introductions because I was, as before, taken after school to start my new life. They were a young couple, and I was their first child. My new family again lived in the same area as my school, so that part of my life continued as usual, which I was very pleased about, although the park was no longer on route to school in the mornings.

Within days of being there, and now becoming quite savvy to people and their personalities, I was aware that something was wrong here.

I got on well with the new father figure in my life, he was funny and laughed out loudly a lot, and I liked it. He had a stubbly ginger beard and not a lot of hair on his head and was originally from London and had a thick east end accent, but the jealousy from my new foster mother became very apparent, very quickly. Whenever it was just the two of us, she would rage through the two-bedroom basement flat, shouting and slamming things and telling me I was an impossible child and that she was hoping for a girl.

She was very slim, with short spiky plum hair and she was never ready for anything unless she was wearing full makeup and false lashes, looking back she did rather have the look of Marti Caine about her.

I remember her always being very tanned and always having a cigarette on the go.

She hated me, and it was so obvious to see, she would either not talk to me when we were home alone, or she would scream at me when I pushed the boundaries.

There seemed to be no acknowledgement from her that I needed to be looked after, I would get up in the morning, her husband would have already left for work as they had a small convenience store across town, and she would be in bed. No attempt at engaging with me would be made, and she would still be there when I closed the front door and headed off to school a little later. Often, she would be sunbathing in the garden when I returned, again the urge to get up and look after the child in front of her never seemed to get hold of her, unless she needed me to go to the shops for some more cigarettes. I would often grab a sandwich and head back out. I was only with them for about three months, through the summer, so the weather was usually good and being out at the park or on the seafront always seemed to be a better option than being ignored or screamed at by her.

Sometimes she would lock me in my bedroom which was at the back of the flat and then she would sit in the lounge and ignore my banging on the doors and my pleads to go to the toilet. It was dreadful; she hated her husband taking an interest in my day at school when he was there and indeed wasn't keen on me helping them out at the shop at the weekends and as a result, I was often told by her to go and sort out the stock room. She wasn't ready for anyone else to have any of her husbands' attention, and she reminded me of my mum so much.

This placement broke down after I told my social worker that I would run away unless he removed me and so, for a few weeks I was sent back to the children's home.

....

My new and final foster family lived in a small town in the East Sussex countryside, which meant this time I had to leave Brighton. I was so angry about this because although my family life in Brighton had been less than ideal, I knew the place well, it was my home in every sense, and I was happy wandering the streets, playing in the parks or reading and drawing on the beach. Although I no longer lived with my sister, the thought of not even being in the same town as her was terrifying but again I had no say in any of it. I had memories in those streets and parks as well as friends, and now I was being moved to a place I had never heard of.

The couple lived in a quiet Cul De Sac, the house was a semi-detached 3-bedroom home, and all the houses looked the same, all brown bricked and brown front doors.

Adam was the father, the dominating, control freak head of the family. He stood at over 6-foot-tall, and his hair was fair in colour, and although he was thinning on top, he had a long mullet at the back, he had a pathetic attempt of a beard and spoke with a slight lisp. I soon got to learn that he also enjoyed walking around the house naked.

His wife, a good 15 years younger, was Deirdre. She was a small dumpy woman with a mass of brown frizzy hair on her head, and she reminded me of the cartoon character from Crystal Tipps and Alistair.

She was very welcoming to me; her voice was soft but high pitched.

They had two sons of their own, one was two years old and the other just a baby, less than a year old. My room was the box room at the front of the house, and I was told I would be attending the local Comprehensive school. Adam ran the local car dealership with his slightly older brother, and Deidre was a stay at home mum, her workload now increased with my arrival.

My time at the large comprehensive school was difficult, and I was bullied for being the new boy and then bullied further for being the only kid in the class that didn't live with his real family.

It was very unlike today, now it seems like many of my kids' friends live in various multicoloured and diverse family set ups. I hated it there.

I didn't do well in lessons, and I rebelled against everything. I used to have to change my walk home on most days to avoid a small gang of four or more boys that would get great pleasure from throwing my rucksack over some random garden fences, while reminding me that no one loved me and I had no family. I didn't make any friends, and I was miserable, I often cried when I left the house to head for school. I missed Brighton, I missed my sister, and I hated my new life.

The rules at home were entirely different for me than those for their sons, which did nothing but remind me that I was not part of this family. They were cuddled and played with, and I wasn't. Once, after telling Adam about a particularly bad day at school, standing there in floods of tears, I reached out for a hug, and he looked at me with a disgusted look on his face and turned his back on me.

There was no nurturing, and again I was never cuddled, the only physical contact was when Adam would smack me around the head for upsetting Deirdre. He was continuously moaning at me and telling me about the teenage girl that they had fostered before me, and how much he missed her.

Years later, after they had moved to the Isle of Wight, they had both gotten heavily involved in the local Methodist Church. Adam had a musical background, so soon got known, running the choir and then creating a youth club.

When at home in the school holidays, I was expected to attend church, which I didn't mind, as well as run the tuck shop at the youth club. Maybe because of what I was experiencing at boarding school, I quickly picked up on what I felt was an unhealthy relationship growing between Adam and a girl of about 13 years old. I noticed the sly winks and smiles that he would give the girl when others were around, the way he would walk a little too closely as he passed her, so that he could secretly brush against her, or place his hands on her shoulders as if he was preventing a collision with her. I picked up on these as they were tactics that Andy used during the busy school hours in the communal areas to keep me under his control.

On one youth club evening, I walked into one of the church halls back rooms and I was sure I had just caught the girl quickly jumping up from Adam's lap. Nothing was said by anyone, and I never witnessed anything again, I was only 14 years old myself, and after that, I wasn't expected to attend church or run the youth club tuck shop again.

In my mid-twenties, I tracked Deirdre down and spoke to her on the phone, and I quickly updated her on what had been happening, how I was now living in Bournemouth and that I had a relationship with my mum. For some reason I decided to come out to her too and tell her I was gay. I asked her about Adam and her, and she told me they were divorced and before I could control my mouth I enquired.

"Was it because of what he was doing with that young girl?" she didn't reply, she swiftly ended the call, promising to call me the following week. I never heard from her again.

……………………………………………..

I got on well with Deirdre, and when Adam wasn't around, we would enjoy each other's company. We would sing to Queen and Abba together, and sometimes she would allow me to watch Dallas with her when Adam was out in the evening. I was very fond of her and started to think of her as my new mum, so it was a surprise when Adam would shout at me and tell me off for upsetting his wife again that day! I later found out that what was really happening was Deirdre was upset and scared by Adam's controlling behaviour and when, in fits of tears, instead of telling her bully the truth, it was safer for her to blame me for her pain. I get it, I understand why she did it, and I forgive her.

It wasn't long until my placement at the school was breaking down. My social worker and Adam were called to a meeting where they were informed I was being expelled.

I ended up hardly ever attending school. I would leave the house every day, with my packed lunch and head off towards the bus stop. I was desperately unhappy there, and the bullying never stopped, so I stopped going.

After leaving the house in the morning, I would walk into the small town and head down towards the railway line. Running alongside the tracks, there was a river where I would pitch up with my little fishing rod, that I kept hidden there in a bush along with a small plastic container of pink larvae, and fish. I would watch the trains go past that were heading to Brighton, the home I really missed.

I would watch the blurred faces of the passenger's whizz by. Hoping to catch a glimpse of my sister, or perhaps, even my parents. I would call out to the trains. "Say Hello to Brighton for me" I would yell, but the thundering track noise would swallow my small voice.

I remember, a day or two after the school meeting, while sitting in my bedroom, listening to Adam making it very clear to my social worker in the lounge beneath me, that as I had been expelled, there was no way I would be able to stay with them any longer. I felt so relieved when I heard this, and I remember being happy and excited, as I knew this would mean I would be taken back to Brighton, possibly back to St Anne's.

I crept out on to the landing to try and hear more of what was being said, Adam had now stopped talking as the social worker was saying something. She was quieter than him, and I found it difficult to hear her.

I lay on the floor; my left ear pressed to the carpet, I thought I had heard her say something about how it would be better for me to stay with them as I had already experienced a lot of upheaval. Her voice was very muffled, the response, however, was very clear to hear as Adam gave a loud and blunt NO!

As the conversation continued, I moved over to the stairs and sat at the top; the lounge door was almost closed, just a small crack allowed for the sound to escape. I tried to suppress my breathing. In an attempt to hear more, I crept down another stair, and then I heard the soft voice of my social worker say the words, boarding school.

CHAPTER FOUR

I was very excited, it was a sunny bright morning, and I was heading to see the new school I was to attend after being expelled from the hell that was the Comprehensive school.

We drove along the country lanes in the bright green Citroen that belonged to my social worker, and every pothole was felt as we bounced along at speed, the car creaked and shook as it shot around corners.

It had been agreed at the meeting the week before that, if I attended a boarding school, I would be able to return to Deirdre and Adam's for some of the school holidays. The half terms, half of the summer holiday and weekends would be spent at school. With promises of a life in the countryside and stories of the working farm that they had at the school, I was happy to go along with this new change, as well as being pleased that it meant I would see a lot less of Adam.

My social worker, Maria, a petite Spanish woman, was speaking to me as the colours of the countryside swept passed me. My excitement was evident to see, and she was desperately trying to calm me down a little, but the next chapter of my life was beginning, and that was all I was able to focus on.

We rounded a corner of the country lane, and a massive, majestic gateway welcomed us.

With dominating stone pillars and ornate black iron gates that were already opened, we were beckoned into my new life.

The long gravel driveway was lined with large well-established trees, the mass of golds, reds, browns, and oranges from their autumnal leaves fed my hungry eyes, the trees lined both sides as we headed towards our destination. I looked around, left to right and out of the back window, I spotted sheep, cattle and a couple of lakes as we headed on, the excitement in my body, now mixed with the anxiety of the unknown.

Finally, the car started to slow down as we came to the end of our journey, the driveway circled round in front of the building.

The large stately 500-year-old country manor, loomed over us blocking out the light from the Sun.

The front was mainly covered with Ivy, the lead windows, many covered with the intrusive plant, offered little more for us to see. Maria looked over at me, reassuring me that everything was going to be OK.

We got out of the car and headed towards the door. It was large and wooden and in the centre was a huge iron door knocker in the shape of a clenched fist, Maria lifted it up and let it drop, she repeated this three times, and we waited, but no one came.

After a while Maria was becoming agitated, checking her watch, then her diary and trying to peer through one of the dark windows, we both jumped a little when from behind us came a man's voice, loud, joyous and very posh.

"Ah there you are, welcome, welcome," the portly man said, his hand stretched out to us as he continued to approach.

He was wearing green wellies, brown corduroy trousers and a checked shirt that just about covered his rotund belly. His sleeves were rolled up past his elbows and, in his other hand, he had a shepherd's crook. A thick mane of greying hair was a mess on top of his head. He had a pipe hanging out of the corner of his mouth, held in by clenched teeth, there were six dogs, of various breeds, running along beside him, 3 of them were huge Saint Bernard dogs.

I stepped behind my social worker for protection, and the farmer in front of us let out a booming laugh, placing his pipe inside his trouser pocket.

"Now don't you worry yourself, they are all completely harmless" he offered.

I liked him instantly, I liked his friendly manner, and I loved the dogs, all 6 of them came bounding up to me and soon I was being sniffed, licked and nudged from every direction.

With introductions out of the way, our host, the schools' Headmaster, named Gerald, gave us a tour of the building.

The interior was every bit as impressive as the outside, wood panelled walls, ornate ceilings and sweeping carved stairways.

Some of the rooms were occupied by other kids, similar ages as myself, all boys, studying as it was a school morning. All the teachers greeted me in the classes we visited, and my excitement continued to build. Not one of the boys was wearing a school uniform, and none of the teachers were in suits.

The grounds, we were told, were a massive 64 acres with two large lakes and a stream, surrounded by bluebell woods. The school ran a working farm, and the boys were welcomed to take part in it if they wished to. There were pigs, sheep, goats and Highland cattle as well a 6 Jersey cows. There were stables, a garage for tractors and dumper trucks and two outdoor tennis courts, at the front of the building was a perfectly laid croquet lawn overlooking the trout lakes, it was a beautiful place.

Two cottages also stood on the grounds, and we were told one was where the English teacher lived with his wife and kids and the other was currently empty. Just up from them were a series of small outbuildings, one was converted into the biology lab, while the other was the art studio. There was also a sizeable walled vegetable garden and a dirty unused outside swimming pool. To me, it all was just amazing.

At the end of the tour, we found ourselves back at the green Citroen, the headmaster bid us farewell and headed back towards the farm. As we drove back down the driveway, Maria asked me what my thoughts were and whether I would be happy there.

I told her how excited I was, how amazing it was, and I confirmed that I was delighted to start my new adventure there. My face ached from the smiling as we, once again, bounced along the long driveway towards the gates. All my yearnings to stay in Brighton had been diminished.

If only I had known then, that the years I would spend at this school would leave me with emotional and physical scars that would last a lifetime.

CHAPTER FIVE

2013

The uncomfortable silence was broken by the squeaking of the tarnished bronze hinges, as the door for courtroom one was opened for me. I took a deep breath to steady myself and twisted my wedding ring on my finger for comfort, I told Kevin in my head that I loved him, but really, I was reminding myself that whatever was about to happen, that I was loved by him and therefore safe. I stepped into the room.

A warm musty, slightly damp smell hit my nostrils as I stepped into the courtroom, and several heads turned to face me momentarily.

The DC in my case was a young woman with a friendly smiling face, her hair as always was pulled back into a tight bun, my barrister, a rather stern looking man, offered me a reassuring, sympathetic smile as the court usher led me to the witness box. As I stepped in, I was given whispered instructions as to how I could sit down now but must stand up when the judge entered. A clear plastic cup of water and a small square box of white tissues were placed in front of me. I looked down, knowing that when I looked up, I wouldn't be able to avoid seeing the monster from my past.

This was my second time at court, the last trial, some nine months previously, had been incredibly emotional and challenging for me. At that time, I had accepted something that is called Special Measures, which are provisions that help vulnerable and intimidated witnesses give their best evidence in court. For me, this meant that a screen was put up to the right of me to protect me from having to make eye contact with the man that was on trial of abusing and raping me as a child all those years ago at boarding school.

The verdict, after two weeks, had been that of a hung jury, the 12 jurors had been unable to agree after the facts had been presented to them, and all the witnesses had been questioned.

When I was told this, I knew why, it was because I knew I had not represented myself well. I hadn't been able to get across all the facts. My time in the box had been ended prematurely due to my emotional response to being questioned and judged.

I had underestimated how difficult it was going to be to have a stranger call me a liar while 12 other strangers looked on, watching my every movement, listening to my every word, reading my facial expressions and writing down things about me that I couldn't see.

I had also underestimated how difficult it was going to be to have to stand in the same room as the man who had raped and abused me, over a period of four years from the age of 11, some 35 years previously.

Although he had been brought into the room after I had been seated behind the screen, I had heard the door creak open for him, and I listened to his feet scuffling along the floor and the chair being pulled back. He coughed to clear his throat. My body had reacted by becoming overcome with anxiety and fear as my mind sent me back to those dark nights when he would creep into the dormitory to satisfy himself. I simply fell apart.

At the first trial, my body had started to shake so badly that I was relieved to have a chair to sit back on, my left leg shook at a great speed and a pain shot through the back of my shoulders and neck.

I looked towards my barrister and the DC, hoping for support but the screen was blocking them from my view as they too were sat down.

I wanted to be home, with my husband and children, I wanted to run, I wanted to be anywhere but there in that box. I didn't want to feel as I did right then, which was as the scared 11-year-old boy that I had been. The jurors came in, I looked over to them, a mixture of sexes and ages, some glanced at me, and some didn't, I felt judged immediately, super sensitive to the anxiety raging through my body.

My sister was sat up in the public gallery, but again I couldn't see her. Kevin, my husband, was out in the main foyer, waiting for his time to be questioned. I began to cry, a deep feeling of pity and sadness for them both grew inside of me, as I knew that they were going to hear about the dark filth that I had endured as a child, the penetrating abuse, the violent rape. Everything that I had tried to protect them from for so long.

A male voice told everyone to rise, as I stood I saw the judge walk into the room, everyone was seated again.

My body was so tight with stress, my mouth dry, my lips stuck to my teeth, within minutes my cup of water had been drained.

When the questioning had begun my emotions took control, and I lost control. My distress was evident to see, and the judge stopped the questioning. Once the accused had been moved from the courtroom, I was taken to a quiet room, and my sister was brought to me.

She hugged me tightly, and my body heaved, from the depth of my being something felt like it physically shifted and crawled its way up through me. A deep groan rose from my gut and escaped through my mouth, and I gasped for air, I couldn't catch my breath, I had no control over what was happening, as something was escaping, something had risen that I had kept buried for so long. As I felt it leave my body, I cried, I sobbed, and I shook.

My sister, the court usher and the DC were all talking to me, reassuring me, trying to comfort me and calm me but I couldn't stop. As I cried, I realised I was grieving. I was crying for the boy that I was, for the boy that again was not being listened to, I was crying for the boy that had been systematically raped, I was grieving for the boy that I had buried so deep down inside myself for decades. For the boy that I had turned my back on by using my middle name after leaving school, for the boy that I had rejected just as much as my parents had.

....

Once I was calmer and composed I was sent home, and the court case continued without me, it had been agreed that I wouldn't go back, that I was best at home and that the DC would update me every day. I drove home in tears, disappointed with myself and angry for letting my abuser win again. I got back home and slept.

On the day of the verdict I was called and told about the hung jury, I wasn't surprised because I had lost control of myself. I was informed that there could be a retrial if I wanted there to be and that I should think about it over the weekend. Without thinking, without any doubt in my mind, I knew I had to do it again, I had come so far, it was three years since it had been reported to the Police and I wasn't going to stop now.

The retrial was booked, and my everyday life continued for the many months leading up to it.

CHAPTER SIX

2015

The 1st of September was a bright and beautiful day, the sky was clear blue and cloudless, and the air was fresh and invigorating.

I drove to the courts alone, and I had told my sister not to come this time as I didn't want her to experience the emotions again. I didn't want her to have to sit there and watch my ABE interview from July three years previously and be reminded of the events in such detail. Besides, this time I felt stronger, in control and balanced. As Kevin was being called as a witness again, he was unable to come with me.

Knowing what was ahead of me this time gave me great comfort, the previous trial had been so horrendous I felt this time that I knew how bad it could get and was, therefore, better prepared. Once again, I was taken to a quiet room, away from any chance of bumping into anyone and the plan of the day was laid out.

Anxiety still raced through my body, but I felt more in control. Once I was left alone, I closed my eyes, and I tried to relax. I sat in the room, alone, with the morning sun streaming through the large 1970's metal framed windows and I thought about my kids, my life with them and how much I loved them. I breathed in deeply and tried to tame my nerves.

I had instructed everyone that I was not going to have special measures this time around, that I felt I needed to face my abuser and had explained that I had previously thought that the screen had protected him from having to face me more than it had been of any benefit to me. I understood what the screen was for, and I could see why some people would get a lot from it, but for me it had just left me feeling more isolated. It was important to me that he would have to look me in the face.

A voice informed me that the court was ready for me, I opened my eyes and focussed, memories of happier times with my kids and husband dissolved, the court usher was smiling at me.

As we left that little piece of sanctuary, I heard the boing of the tannoy system and a crackled voice asking everyone to do with my case to go to courtroom one.

As I walked the dark corridor, I shuddered as if touched by death himself. The fear was once again pulsing through my veins as my anxiety taunted me about how bad things were about to get. It wasn't long until I found myself standing outside the courtroom door again.

I took a deep breath and stepped in.

……………………………………………..

To my left, as I entered, there was the witness box, following my line of sight around I saw the court clerks at their desks and the stenographer, the judges' seat, higher than everyone else, was behind them.

Directly opposite the witness box was the jurors seating area. To my right, just in front of me, sat my barrister and the DC and next to them the defence barrister, behind me was the box for the accused.

As I was led to the witness box, I turned and saw the accused behind the glass wall surrounding his stand.

He stood there in a grey suit, he was larger in build than the 30 plus years ago, and his hair was short and grey. He avoided my eyes, staring directly ahead of himself. Sitting next to him was a custody officer.

The public gallery was directly above the accused. His wife sat there alone.

Once the jury had been sworn in, and the judge was ready, the questioning began. The previous day the jurors had watched the ABE video, and I was first to be questioned.

My barrister started, leading the trial by asking me questions based on the facts, photographs of the school building were shown to everyone in the courthouse, and I was asked to explain the layout of the building in as much detail as possible. I had lived there for five years and knew it well. I pointed to windows, naming what each room was, my dormitory, the headmasters' room, the matrons' room, kitchen, art room, bathrooms and finally the bedroom where much of the rape and abuse took place.

I was asked to explain the proximity of that room to the dormitory and how long it took to get from one to the other.

I felt calm, I knew what I was saying couldn't be disputed, the layout of the building was something that all the witnesses from back then would agree on.

My dormitory was in the central part of the building, on the top floor, in the attic area. It was large, and there were three sets of bunk beds for six boys. I only shared the room with two other boys, so we each had a bunk bed. My bed was on the left as you entered the room, it was the first you saw, and I slept on the bottom mattress. Behind the door, to the right, were the other two bunk beds, then three desks next to the windows which overlooked the fields. The view was incredible, and I would often sit there in the afternoon taking it all in, directly below was the lawn area, and there was usually a dog or four down there with some boys. Just after that lay a field with an electric fence surrounding it, in the area were the magnificent Scottish Highland cattle with their enormous horns and long red hair, alongside them were the Jersey cows, with their bulging udders. We would help hand milk them at the end of the day, providing the school with milk, cheese, and butter, often the goats would be in the same field too, grazing away. To the left of it was the start of the bluebell woods and the boggy lake with its tiny bubbling stream. A pathway started there that went right around the grounds, taking you past another lake, two waterfalls and up through the tranquil woods. My favourite place to be. To the right of my bedroom view was a greenhouse and beyond that the old unused outdoors swimming pool that was teeming with crested newts, ripe for catching and taken to our dormitories in old ice cream containers, much to the horror of the school cleaner who would rerelease them when we were all in class.

Across the landing was an identical dormitory but with two sets of bunk beds and two single beds up near the windows, this room also only had three boys in it. In between the two dormitories were two separate bedrooms, each taken by two older boys. Also leading off the landing was the fire exit door that led to the massive iron staircase that took you down to the driveway.

On the floor below us, to the left was the head master's bedroom, a bathroom, and the English teachers room. To the right was a large hall area where a vast Loom stood collecting dust next to the second fire escape door. In all the years I was there I had never seen it used. Opposite the Loom was the matrons' room, she was lucky enough to have a balcony which overlooked the lawn area outside. Back in the hallway was a wall of built-in cupboards, in which were stored the towels, blankets and the bedding for the whole school. The history teachers room and a single toilet were also on this landing, then down five stairs, to the left, was a bathroom, and a little further was the shower room at the top of a flight of stairs where I had been violently raped. To the right, opposite the shower room were three other rooms. One was an unused dormitory, while the other two were single bedrooms, one taken by the cleaner and the other by another old pupil who was now teaching geography at the school. Although the only non-abusive male member of staff, he knew what was going on and did nothing to stop it.

Following on through the house, down three stairs, and to the left was a steep flight of stairs that led into the area known as The Cottage. At the bottom, there was a room and bathroom which was occupied by the biology teacher and his wife, there was also a single toilet. Then directly ahead, at the bottom of the stairs was another flight of stairs which led up to a corridor. There were two separate rooms on this floor, which were to the left, and at the end of the passage stood the grubby, imposing door that opened into the place where the rapist lived.

....

The judge thanked me for the thorough description of the building, and my barrister asked me to describe the first time I had met my abuser.

I went on and explained that it was at the beginning of a new year, a new term and the school had moved premises. Although most of the moving had been completed in the Christmas holidays, when all us boys had come back, the school still wasn't quite ready.

With the education term being delayed we all helped moving beds, cupboards, and desks into the correct rooms. Some old pupils, boys that were now men, who had been at the school years before, had come down to help with the move, and that was when I first met him.

Andy was large in build, overweight and standing at 6 feet 4 inches; he towered over the small 11-year-old boy that I was. The headmaster introduced some of us younger boys to him and his brother, who was also there. We all helped them with moving some boxes. Andy was funny, friendly and approachable. He laughed with us younger boys, picking us up to reach high places and supplied us with cans of coke and bags of crisps to reward us for our hard work and to encourage us to sit on his lap and allow him to tickle the back of our necks.

My barrister asked me to describe the first-time things had changed between us? When had Andy changed the dynamics? When did the abuse first start?

I took a mouthful of water; the plastic cup had already been filled up twice before. The inside of my mouth felt swollen due to it being so dry. My lips stuck together, my attempt to moisten them with a lick of my tongue was useless as my body had ceased producing any saliva.

I started to explain that one night, about eight weeks into term time, I must have been woken by a whisper or a slight prod because as my senses awoke, I could hear a man's deep but hushed voice talking to me, saying my name. I didn't move for a moment as I tried to work out what was happening and where this voice was coming from? I turned my head to the left to look towards the other bunk beds and was shocked to see that Andy was kneeling beside me, his face very close to mine.

I was startled at first but not afraid because I already thought of him as my friend, I offered him a sleepy smile. He asked if I was OK and I replied. The top half of his body was leaning into me, and the side of my mattress was depressed, sending me closer to him.

He was propped up on his right elbow, and his left hand was stroking my hair. I didn't ask him what he wanted, and I don't recall that ever entering my mind. He continued to whisper to me. He asked me how I was? If I had had a good day? He also told me I was a good boy and that I was special to him. His friend.

It was while he was talking to me that I noticed something was happening, something that I had never experienced before. He was now sitting up a little straighter, no longer resting on his right elbow and his left hand was now underneath my blanket and sheet, it was heavy on my crutch, not moving, just there, pressing down on me, on top of my pants, on top of my child cock.

He continued to talk to me, but now I was unable to focus on what he was saying, my head was rushing with my own voice as fear started to pound on the inside of my skull.

I paused and took a sip of water, I looked at the jury and told them how I had wondered, "What was going on? What was he doing?".

My eyes stung with tears as I stood in the witness box reliving the horror in front of so many people.

I went on to explain how that night I was embarrassed and that I had closed my eyes, his hand was heavy on me, the weight unwanted. I talked about how he started to rub my private parts through my pants and how he had then been startled and quickly removed his hand and kept still as the boy on the top bunk opposite me stirred. I went on telling them that once he felt it was safe, he had lent in again and told me I was a good boy and that then he had left the room.

"I didn't know what to do?", I said, "When he left I rolled over and thought about what had just happened."

Memories had then flooded my head as I lie in my bed trying to figure out what had just happened. Memories of the first time I had joined the school, it was to be the last term at the original property, and another older boy, an ex-pupil that was living there had befriended me. As I hardly knew anyone at the time, I was grateful for the attention.

He was very artistic and loved music, he had shoulder length blond hair and was quite effeminate in his mannerism. He started to invite me to his room in the long afternoon breaks to listen to his LP's. His room was always very thick with the aroma of cannabis, patchouli oil, and incense.

He was softly spoken, gentle and again, as Andy was to do in the future, he treated me to cans of drink and sweets.

I lay in my bottom bunk and remembered that he had a massive wooden four poster bed which we were all encouraged to relax on when listening to music. There were a couple of other boys that also used to go to his room regularly in the afternoons. Then one day, when three of us, two boys and the adult, where laying on the bed listening to Elton John sing about a yellow brick road, he had reached out to me as I lay on my back looking at the cover of the LP. He had started to rub my cock through my corduroy trousers. I hadn't moved or shown that I was aware, and to this day I have no idea why? He then began to rub me a little harder and laughing in a girlish giggly manner between the drags of another spliff.

"Look," he said to the other boy on the bed.

"His little dick has gone hard, how cute is that"

I looked down to where his hand was, and I saw that I was hard, I didn't know what had happened as I had never had an erection before. The reality switch snapped on in my head, and I got up and ran out of the room.

Over the coming weeks, I avoided his invites and his reassurances that I shouldn't have run out that afternoon.

When I woke up the next morning, after Andy's' late-night visit, confused and scared, I lay still under my blanket until I heard the other two boys go down to breakfast before I got up. My bed was wet, and my pants were cold and smelt. I realised that I had wet my bed, the first time in many years.

I pulled the blanket over the stain and ran down to the bathroom and washed. I pulled my pants off and cleaned myself with a flannel, trying to remove the smell of urine, the memory of the time before, with the other adult, shouted inside my head, telling me that this behaviour must be normal, as it had now happened twice and by two different people.

I cried as I washed, ashamed of myself for wetting the bed, and ashamed that I had allowed it to happen again. I threw my pants away in the bathroom bin, stuffing them to the bottom, covering them with old tissue, worried someone would see them.

My barrister asked me if that was the only time that Andy had come to the dormitory at night? I told him no. I went on to explain that it became regular and that on a couple of weekends when I was there alone, because the other boys had gone home to their families, he would masturbate me and get me to rub his erection through his jeans until a damp patch appeared. My barrister thanked me and invited me to sit back down.

………………………………………………..

His barrister, a stout, older man who reminded me of Mole from Wind in The Willows, stood up, he looked over at me, looking down and over his glasses, possibly an attempt to unnerve me further. I again took in more water and waited, I stayed sitting.

He began by stating that he was not there to upset me but to get to the facts. To disclose the truth, whatever that was and to make sure the jury was only presented with what really had happened, if indeed anything had.

He cleared his throat, looked briefly down at the paperwork in front of him and then back up at me, his hands clasped on to the chest of his gown.

"Mr. Spencer, this is all a lie, isn't it?" he asked, I stood steadfastly and confident, this was the second time this guy had cross-examined me, and I was better prepared than I had been previously.

"No" I replied

"Well, come on Mr Spencer, I was hardly expecting you to say yes, but we will get to that later because you and I know that this is all a lie". He shifted on his feet slightly without breaking eye contact, "The claims that you are making are preposterous, aren't they?"

I leaned forward, placing my mouth closer to the small thin microphone in front of me.

"No" I replied again, louder this time.

"OK, let us try something different, everyone agrees that you knew my client, there is no disputing that, but let's get to the point of dates."

My throat became tight and my mouth dried up again. I took in more water, I thought I knew what he was about to say as he had questioned me about this at the previous l, but I was wrong.

"Since the last trial Mr Spencer, have you made any amendments to your statement?"

"No" I replied

"None at all?"

"No, none," I said.

He went on to ask if I had made any adjustments to the timeline and reminded me and informed the jury that at the previous trial it had been unclear exactly how old I had been and what the dates were.

"I am correct am I not? that there was some confusion?" he licked his finger and turned a page of his file.

"Yes, I guess so" I answered

"Yet you've not changed this?"

I could feel the anger building up inside myself, the smug look on the barrister's face, and his cocky attitude was making me mad.

"I didn't change them because as far as I know, and I believe, I am correct about them, to the best of my knowledge."

"Quite" he smiled at the jury

Exact dates had been difficult for me as it had been 30 plus years since I had met Andy.

His barrister then started to bombard me with questions, again and again, he fired them at me, giving me very little time to respond.

I began to panic, which he noticed, and he continued to try to slip me up, confuse me and to get me to change my story.

"So, what year was this?", he asked, quickly followed by "and how old do you claim you were?"

I looked at the jury and explained again that it had been decades ago. That due to growing up in the care system I didn't have anyone to go to, to ask when did this happen? Or what age I was when I started at the school?

I had always believed and understood from my memories that I was ten years old when I went to the Boarding School. But here, now, while standing in front of a room of strangers, I was being told I was wrong, that Andy hadn't moved into the school when I had claimed. His barrister was telling us all that it had been a year later, that I had been a year older and that this showed clearly that I was not telling the truth.

My thoughts swam around my head, crashing into each other, the barrister's voice, my inner voice, clashing, causing my head to pound.

I knew I was right though, and I knew that he had moved in at the beginning of term after we had all helped to finish off the school move. I knew this for sure because a few of us had helped him to move his belongings into his room and over the following few days, we had also helped him to decorate. An apple white colour, a very pale green, had been used for the walls and then posters of windsurfing, a hobby that he apparently shared with his brothers, were put up.

His barrister kept on at me about the dates and how I was wrong. I didn't know what else to say, I just kept giving the same answer, the truth, but he wouldn't let go.

I turned to the Judge, "I don't know what else to say, your Honour, this is the truth, and he won't let go of it".

The Judge offered me a reassuring smile, "You are right Mr Spencer" he said

He addressed the barrister, telling him that I had answered and that he should move on with his questioning.

"Whatever age I was, I was still a child, and he was fucking me" I shouted out at the barrister.

I waited for the questions to start about the perverse sexual acts that I had been made to do, the fucking, the sucking and the coming to my dormitory, but he said nothing about it.

"Now Mr Spencer we have all heard that your childhood had been tough for you, your Mother was an alcoholic, and your father was hardly ever around. It was a violent relationship I understand, which led to the breakup of their marriage and you were placed in the care system at the age of 6 or 7 years old, is this correct?"

"Yes" I replied

"and am I correct in saying that you had several unsuccessful foster placements."

I replied again with a "Yes."

"So, by the time you had been placed at the boarding school, it would be fair for me to say that you didn't trust adults? You had no reason to, and you had been let down continually for many years by many adults".

Again, I agreed with what he had said

"and then you met my client who was very friendly wasn't he?" he didn't wait for an answer and continued.

"He was friendly to everyone, adults, and children and you enjoyed his company". This was not a question, rather more a fact he was giving.

"Now we all know you were alone, scared and untrusting but you soon became attached to my client, in fact, some would say obsessed with him, wouldn't they?"

This time he paused so I jumped in with an answer before he could move on.

"Yes, he was very friendly towards me and some of the other boys". My voice was croaky, my head continued to pound.

"But I wasn't obsessed with him; you make it sound like I stalked him"

"Well," he laughed and faced his audience of 12 offering them a victorious smile before turning back to me, "That is exactly what I am saying"

I took in more water, readying myself for a battle, this was the second time this man had questioned me, ripped into me, humiliated me and called me a liar and there was no way I was going to let that happen again. My body tingled with strength, with power, with self-respect and I responded.

"He was my friend, or at least that is what I thought at the time. He would seek me out, ask me to help him cook, to wash his work van and to clean his room and he would pay me for this, give me his loose change and buy me cans of pop."

I shifted my feet, spacing them a little, getting a firmer stance, I looked at the jury and continued.

"You have to remember I was very young, 10 or 11 years old, I looked completely different then, I was a small child, a loner. No one cared about me, no one took any interest in me before I went to the school and yes, the attention I got was exciting, the comics, the music, being allowed to watch TV in his room, it made me feel special and important."

I paused and looked towards Andy, and his eyes met mine briefly. I moved my gaze to the jury and continued.

"But with that came the sex, the abuse, the violence". My voice started to break, and my eyes betrayed my inner strength as tears began to run down my cheeks.

I remember his barrister trying to speak, but I cut him off. "You have to let me speak" I barked at him.

I told everyone listening how part of my life at the school was great, working on the school farm, the woods, the fishing lake, I loved all that, but behind closed doors, it was a different story.

The school was a cesspit of pain, of abuse and lies. Many teachers at the school had their favourite boys, and they would spoil them, treat them, spend time alone in their rooms with them and no one ever questioned it. The History teacher, the English and Math teachers, the Head Master and the Art teacher, they all either had boys, or there were rumours that they had previously been linked to some.

"It wasn't spoken about as being wrong; it just happened, it was the norm at this place," I told the jury.

I continued to tell my audience of 12 that there were two female members of staff, the Matron, and the cleaner, and they too knew what was going on and did nothing. No one cared about anyone in that place, during the day it was lessons, cooking, fun, games, laughs, and jokes. But at night, after 10 pm the place was dark, cold and quiet, the peace was broken by the sounds of doors creaking open and closed as the adult males gorged on the boys.

"I thought that the sex that was demanded from me was normal, I knew it was what the other boys were doing with some of the teachers, so I didn't fight it." My face was wet with my tears as I looked at the jury, two of the women had concern written over their faces, and I dared to hope that at that moment that they believed me.

"But it didn't happen did it". The barrister interrupted me, probably also aware that some members of the jury were sympathetic to what I was sharing.

"Yes, you are right that my client was friendly towards you, but he didn't single you out for any preferential treatment. As you have said earlier he was a popular person, everyone liked him, isn't that correct?"

I wasn't sure if I was supposed to answer, but he continued before I had the chance to conclude.

"It was you that wanted more, and it was you that made advances towards my client and, rightly so, he turned you down as he was an adult and you a child."

Anger whelmed up inside me, what was he saying? That I, a young boy had made sexual advances towards an adult? That I was a pervert? That I wanted to be fucked by this man? I could feel that I was about to lose control of myself and I gripped the sides of the witness box tightly.

"I put it to you, Mr Spencer, that you were a child spurned and this is some kind of revenge, that you have held a grudge towards my client for all these years because he didn't prefer you over anyone else, and here we are today because of it."

My stomach turned, and my head spun, I couldn't believe what I was hearing, my right leg began to shake, and I felt like I was going to pass out.

"Mr Spencer, are you OK?" the judge was looking at me, I nodded yes and wiped my eyes.

"Shame on you", I shouted at the barrister, "Shame on you for knowing what he did to me and making out I wanted it". I was now full of rage.

"But I don't know what my client did to you do I Mr Spencer? I only know what you are saying"

I wanted to run, to leave the courtroom, to exit before my time being questioned was over, but I was also determined not to let this man get away with what he had done to me all those years back.

"He singled me out", I shouted. I took a deep breath and started again, "He knew I was the kid at school who had no family to turn to, that I stayed at the school most of the holidays when the other boys went home. I was easy prey for him". The shaking subsided, "He raped me" He would take me to his room and fuck me, a boy, he would never use condoms or lube, just spit, and he would fuck me, bite my back and cum in me and then tell me to leave. He would ram his cock into my mouth and force me to swallow his fucking cum."

The courtroom fell quiet; I remember wishing that my husband Kevin was with me. I looked over at the accused, and he avoided my stare.

"Mr Spencer". The judge was addressing me, "I understand this is very difficult for you and that of course emotions are high, but I must ask you not to use that kind of language in my courtroom."

I apologised, I looked over at the jury and spoke to them directly.

"You have to understand, this isn't part of some big plan of revenge, it wasn't even me that reported it initially". Some of the 12-avoided eye contact with me, looking down at their pads, others, mainly the women, listened, looking directly at me.

I went on to explain how, during our assessment with Barnardo's to be foster carers, I had mentioned that I was abused as a child at the boarding school. I went on to explain how they had told me about their duty of care, which meant they would have to report it to the Local Authority.

I hadn't wanted them to, and I felt that it wasn't their place to talk about my life to others, but I knew I had no choice. I thought that I had moved on from it and the last thing I wanted was Andy and that life infesting the life I now had with Kevin.

I continued to explain that a week later, East Sussex Local Authority contacted me about my disclosure and took some further details over the phone, they encouraged me to report it to the Police, but at that time I refused to.

I looked over at the officer in charge of my case, and she offered me a reassuring nod of her head, I took another sip of water and continued to address the jury.

"After I had spoken to the Local Authority, something had opened inside me, the memories started to come crashing back to me, vivid and upsetting and I started to feel I had to do something."

I went on to tell them that I then contacted the police, and they had sent an officer over to my house to take a statement. I continued that later, I wasn't sure what the timescale was, I had then been contacted by the officer in charge of my case, and I gave my ABE video evidence.

Tears continued to run down my face as I told the jury that I had realised that I needed to report it if I was going to be able to be a good parent to our adopted kids.

"How could I have been a good parent myself and support them through the abuse and neglect that they had endured with their birth families, if I hadn't looked after the boy that I was". I finished.

....

I don't remember his barrister saying much more to me after that, the judge then thanked me for my time and my honesty, and I was dismissed from the courtroom.

In my ABE interview, I had spoken in detail about the progress of the abuse, from touching me at night in my bed, to masturbating me in the dormitory. I had gone on to talk about the collecting me and carrying me to his room, to him then just telling me in the afternoons and early evenings, in front of anyone in earshot, to come to his room later that night.

I described the force of him ramming his erect penis into my small child mouth. How he would make me sit on the edge of his bed, so he could stand in front of me, slightly bending his knees to get into position. The fear of what was happening would dry out my mouth, making his invasion more painful as he stuck to the inside, often causing me to gag.

I was asked in the interview to talk about the anal rape, so I spoke about the first time. When, after he had forced me to have oral sex, he had stripped naked and laid down in the middle of his bed. He had then encouraged me to undress, telling me how special I was and how excited he was. He then made me sit on his fat hairy stomach, my legs either side of him. While talking to me and smiling, he spat on his left hand and wiped the saliva onto the head of his cock before lifting me up on to it and pushing me down, so his hardness ripped into my body.

The pain was unlike anything I had ever experienced, every sense in my body screamed. I tried to pull up, to escape, but with his strength and big hands, he held me where I was with little effort. My stomach turned, I dug my nails into my thighs as he forced himself in harder and faster. My eyes exploded with tears, and I repeated: "No, No, No." I couldn't have been clearer that he was doing this without consent. Through my blurred vision I could see him, his head back, his eyes closed as he enjoyed the torture of my body.

This progressed to me being fucked 6-7 times a week and changed to include mornings before school assembly as well as some late nights. In the mornings, I would, after instruction from him the night before, take him a coffee around 8 am. I would put the coffee on his bedside table, and he would lift the far side of his duvet as a prompt for me to climb in, discarding my clothes on the floor, I would do as instructed.

I would lay on my left side, and he would pull me in close to him and invade my body, using just his spit to lubricate. He would fuck me, and he would ejaculate inside me, and also bite the top of my back as he climaxed. When I was finished with, I would get up, get dressed and leave. This horror went on for years, and he damaged my body physically by tearing me repeatedly inside. The rape became so frequent that my injuries never had time to heal.

During the morning fuck sessions, he would hardly ever speak to me, most times he would utter nothing more than a grunt, but by the time we had all come out of the school assembly, he would be in the communal kitchen, smiling and chatting to others.

Outside of the abuse, he was very kind to me, he was my friend, and protected me from the teasing and bullying that I got from the other boys. He always encouraged me with my school work and seemed to take an interest in what I did.

When I think back now, as a 48-year-old man and revisit the memories of the rape and abuse, I realise that over the years that it was going on he must have raped me well over a thousand times. All unprotected, all without lubrication and all violently. There was never a cuddle or any sign of affections. I now recognise that the nice part of our friendship was just him grooming me.

On one day in a half-term holiday, those of us that were still at the school helped the headmaster down on the farm with building a new pigsty. It was a hot day, and the work was hard, dirty but fun. In the late afternoon when the work was done, and two very happy potbellied pigs were enjoying their new residence, we all went back inside the school.

Andy told me to go to the single shower room and get in the shower but to leave the door unlocked. I did as I was told.

Once I was under the hot water and washing the mud and pig shit off my hands the shower room door opened and my abuser walked in, and he closed it behind him.

He stood there briefly, a white towel, which barely wrapped around him, dropped to the floor and he stepped into the water. The room was full of steam, and he was now standing behind me.

His hands pulled me in closer to him, and the water ran through my hair and then down my face.

He instructed me to give him the bar of carbolic soap that was on the window sill to the right of us, and he began to wash my back and shoulders. I could feel the soap suds running down me as he moved the bar up and down my back, then without warning, he pushed one corner of the bar into my arsehole with a sudden thrust. I remember wincing and pulling away, the pain felt like a knife had been stabbed into me, I was still raw and damaged from the last time. The skin around my anus was always wounded and torn as the rape never really ever eased up. I heard the slapping sound of the soap being lathered up in his hands, and then the bubbles were rubbed into my hole, his fingers probing slightly. I knew then what was going to happen, and my body tensed, readying itself for another invasion.

I squeezed my buttocks hard to try and close any entry point, but he was a lot stronger than me. He wrapped his right arm around my waist and lifted me slightly as well as pushing me into the tiled wall, my toes were barely touching the shower tray as I was now on tiptoe. My body shook as he again raped me with his hard-aggressive erection. His cock tore into me again, and the water offered no lubrication as he entered, the thrusting pushed the soap suds in which stung as he ripped at my insides.

My face was hard up against the wet tiles, and his left hand was on my head as he moved faster and faster, banging my face against the tiles, resulting in a split lip, blood now trailed out of my mouth and down my chin.

It was over in a short space of time, as again, he unloaded inside me. When finished, he turned his back to me and started to wash; it was as if none of it had happened and that I hadn't been there in that tiny shower cubicle just seconds before.

I got out, grabbed my pile of clothes and towel and left. After checking no one was around, I ran into the toilet next door but one, and tried to dry myself.

The inside of my buttocks and the top of my legs throbbed with pain, my bottom lip was swollen and bleeding.

I wiped my bum and in between my cheeks and it stung like hell, I looked at the towel which was now blemished with red streaks from my blood.

Sitting down on the toilet I strained hard to get his sperm out of my body, and it spluttered out of me with my blood. The water in the basin was a mixture of sodden paper, red blood, and his discharge. I sat, naked and cold on the toilet and cried. I waited until I had heard him leave the shower room and I rushed up to my dormitory.

During my time at the school I used to have six monthly reviews where my social worker and foster dad would come and discuss how I was doing at school with the headmaster. I was always invited in for the last 20 minutes or so, but I never really knew what had been discussed before.

On the two reviews in the same year when I was about 13 years old, I had told my social worker before the meetings that a former pupil that lived there was having sex with me. I remember the disappointment by his lack of shock or empathy as he told me he would discuss it in the meeting. I have no idea if he did? I just know that nothing happened and that years later, when I looked, nothing could be found in my case file.

CHAPTER SEVEN

Set on the outskirts of a beautiful Sussex village, the school was established in acres of countryside with a fantastic farm. To anyone looking in as an outsider it would have seemed very idyllic. We milked our cows, we fished our waters and grew all our own vegetables.

However, the truth was that it was a strange and dangerous place, a separate world that you entered once you had crossed over the gate threshold.

It was an environment where there were no rules, no boundaries or love. Where teachers would invite boys back to their rooms, where boys would be asked to sit on adults' laps in communal areas and expected to kiss the headmaster on the cheek, where no one questioned anything.

It was a place where one day at dinner, in front of the whole school, the biology teacher had asked my attacker not to be so loud when fucking me in the room above his; I was 12 or 13 years old at the time, the whole school erupted with laughter, including the headmaster. Again, no one said it was wrong.

It was also the place where, when one of the boys had given himself a tattoo with a needle and some Indian ink.

The same biology teacher in the same dining room at another dinner time, got a Brillo pad and some cleaning powder and scrubbed at this boys' arm until he broke the skin and it bled.

Again, nobody stopped him, but they all laughed about it and cheered on his barbaric behaviour.

By the time I was about 15 years old the abuse had pretty much stopped. I'm not sure if I had gotten too old or had been "replaced" by one of the newer younger boys. Andy was still friendly to me when others were around, but the abuse had reduced.

Sometimes at the weekends, on a Friday or Saturday night, when he would return late from the pub, he would summon me, fuck me, and breathe his beer-soaked breath across my back as he panted and groaned. The fucking would go on longer at these times, probably because of the alcohol in his body numbing the sensation in his cock, and my insides would be damaged further.

Looking back on it I wonder if his lessened interest in me may have been because I had reached puberty.

I had always been tiny for my age and a late developer, so my new hairiness, body odour and acne may have been putting him off. Whatever the reason was, I remember being very grateful for the rest from the ongoing slaughter I had endured for so long.

One evening, not that far away from my 16th Birthday and close to my time at the school coming to an end, he had told me in the kitchen area to go to his room as he had wanted to talk to me and that he also had a Birthday present for me.

Communication between us had pretty much come to an end by this time, and I was no longer going to his room or being raped. He left the kitchen, and I waited a few minutes and followed him up. I wondered, indeed hoped, that I was going to get an apology for the years of abuse.

I knocked on his door and waited for a reply, the door swung open, and he grabbed my top pulling me in. He pushed me on to his bed and told me to get undressed, and he reached for his own belt to release it.

I don't know why but something snapped inside me this time, and I stood back up and told him no.

"You ungrateful fucking cunt," he said to me as he leant in close, he was so close to my face that I felt his spit spray me. He pushed me back on to the bed, but I stood back up straight away.

"Fuck off", I responded and pushed him away, I was a lot bigger and heavier than the 11-year-old boy he had groomed so many years previously, and he staggered backwards slightly. I reached for the door handle to leave the room.

BANG! He pushed me against the door and landed a heavy kick to the back of my legs sending me into the door, and the metal handle jabbed into my ribs, I turned to face him and saw pure anger and hatred written across his red face. His right-hand moved up towards my throat and I kicked out, my foot hit his body, but I had no idea where. I turned, yanking the door open and headed down the corridor.

More verbal abuse was coming my way, I misjudged how far away from me he was, and I stopped to turn and hurl some back, but he was there. Just inches away from me and he punched me in the stomach. I doubled over as he grabbed me, dragging me back towards his room, I lashed out over and over and managed to catch him in the face. He let go of me, so I ran, he was fast behind me and kicked out as I reached the top of the stairs, striking my lower back with his boot and I went hurtling down. I missed the first few steps but hit all the rest and landed at the bottom; he was stood at the top, sweating and puffing away.

"Fucking cunt" he shouted at me.

I got up and ran into the main part of the school and headed straight to the headmasters' room across the landing.

I paused to try and catch my breath and then knocked.

A deep voiced "Enter", permitted me to push the door open, as I did my eyes focussed and I saw the headmaster sitting at the far end of his room by the window, puffing from his pipe, the room was dimly lit by one lamp and a small TV.

He greeted me and asked what I wanted, still stood by the door, with it open behind me, I told him about how for years I had been forced to have sex with Andy. I explained that tonight because I had said no, I had been beaten up and kicked down the stairs. I lifted my top and turned around to show him my back which was pulsing with pain, and I could feel the whelks with my fingers.

The headmaster, the man in charge, the man that had been given responsibility for my welfare by the Local Authority, the man who had been a father figure to me for some many years, laughed out loudly.

I remember his words so well, as he took a drag from his pipe and bellowed the smoke, from behind the stinking cloud he said

"My dear boy, really? You should have come to me years ago, I would have had sex with you too of course, but I would never have beaten you up". I stood there in shock, I didn't know what to say, so I stepped back and closed the door, the next morning nothing was said about it.

CHAPTER EIGHT

2015

After I had finished giving evidence, the other witnesses were called, one was my husband Kevin, who was asked about the last ten years of our life together and about when and how I had disclosed my abuse to him. Kevin had told them that we had both early on in our relationship realised that we had something special, so we invested in each other and talked about our pasts. That was when I had told him what had happened to me, and I also told him because physically I was still damaged by the rape which meant I couldn't do some sexual acts and I was afraid he would leave me because of that.

The other two witnesses were the biology teacher from the school and an ex-pupil who had moved into the school as an adult for a period of time.

I decided to leave and wait at a local café for Kevin; I didn't want to see him being questioned by the perverts' barrister. I didn't trust that my emotions wouldn't get the better of me and I certainly didn't want to hear the lies from the other two, who, at the previous trial, had denied any knowledge of any abuse or violence but did put me in the company of my abuser many times, including in his room, late at night.

Knowing that these two were lying, protecting him, hurt a lot but it didn't surprise me. It reminded me of the boy that I was, that no one listened to or protected.

The following day the accused was to be called to give his evidence, and unlike at the last trial I wanted to be in the gallery, I needed to listen to him, I wanted to hear how he could possibly defend himself. I needed to experience it to be able to heal and move forward eventually.

I woke the next day with a feeling of strength after the first good night's sleep in months. I felt like an oppressive weight that I had carried around for decades had finally had its lid cracked open slightly. That being able to stay relatively composed. As well as getting everything I wanted to say said at court the previous day had helped the slow healing process to start for me, for the pain to begin to be released finally. I headed to the court and sat in the waiting area.

The bright winter sun again flowed in through the dirty windows of the building, lighting up the well-worn frayed public area. My DC and barrister came over to see how I was feeling and told me they would touch base with me later in the morning and then they both disappeared into one of the many small rooms to the side.

I sat there, thoughts crammed into my head about what I would hear that morning, and the beast that is my anxiety started to claw at me deep inside, I closed my eyes to focus, and a calming internal voice told me to breathe and reminded me that he couldn't hurt me anymore.

Voices interrupted my meditation, and I slowly opened my eyes to look for the source. I saw him standing just a few feet away from me with his wife and barrister, his wife looked drawn and pale, and my heart went out to her.

I felt sorry for her because he was destroying her life too. He had lied, hidden a side to him that was dangerous and manipulative. I did not doubt that he was still abusing boys and those weaker than himself. There was no way that raping me all those years ago, had been enough to satisfy his thirst.

When he had been arrested all those years previously, the Police had told me that he was now a senior social worker for vulnerable adults. My stomach had done a flip when I heard this; this man had plainly put himself in an environment where he could continue his secret sordid lust after the closing down of the school.

His barrister saw me looking over at them and quickly they too disappeared into another small room.

A little while later a distorted voice announced that all involved in the case were to head to Courtroom one again. I made my way to the gallery, closely followed by his wife, we were sat at opposite ends, about 12 discoloured fixed seats separated us. There was no one else there.

Once the judge and the jury had been seated, and he was in the witness box his barrister began to question him. Questions about whether he knew me? Whether he was at the school and whether we spent time together were all confirmed. His voice was loud and dominating, and I recognised the arrogance from all those years ago, he looked up a couple of times towards his wife.

"Is it true that Mr Spencer would go into your private room?"

"Yes, it is, but so did many other boys and not just my room but also other teachers." He shifted on his feet and took a sip of water.

"At night too?". his barrister continued

"No not at night, evenings, yes but not nights."

"Early mornings?" the questions continued

"Absolutely not!" he was firm with his answer this time.

"But we have heard from other witnesses in this trial that Mr Spencer often took you coffee in the mornings before the school's assembly."

Although it wasn't a question he answered. "That is absolutely not true". He turned to face the judge as he answered.

His barrister continued by asking questions about the boy that I was. Was I a needy child? Did I seek out his attention? And Did he ever feel uncomfortable with my need to be liked?

I sat above them becoming increasingly angry inside. I watched as these two men made out that an 11-year-old boy was somehow a sexual predator to a full-grown man. I kept myself composed, not showing the anger I felt, or indeed verbalising it, every now and then members of the jury would look up at me, I guess to see what my reaction was to his statements.

His barrister continued questioning him, did he ever buy me gifts or give me money, did he ever seek me out for company? All of it he denied.

My barrister was next to question him; I shifted forward in my seat a little to get ready for what was about to happen. I hoped he would rip him apart and show the jury precisely who he was.

"It is true, is it not, that you had sex with my client, that you orchestrated being alone with him and that you raped him."

Again, "Absolutely not", was the response. Andy's forehead was now wet with sweat.

"Isn't it also true that you preyed on my client for years to come, that you pretended to be his friend to satisfy yourself."

"Absolutely not!" came his reply once again, he shifted on his feet, looked up towards his wife, then to the jury and then took a sip of water.

The questioning went on; he had admitted that he had been an appropriate adult on the school boating holiday. This appeared to confuse the judge, as earlier, he had also claimed that he only lived there and had nothing to do with the running of the school. Another lie. He stuttered and hesitated when asked why I knew that he had been circumcised. The judge had jumped in again at this point for clarification. Andy had said everyone knew that he was. The Judge had then asked, was it communal showers at the school? Andy had said no; the judge had continued that he didn't understand how everyone would know that he had been circumcised?

I remember feeling disappointed that his questioning had been so quick and less aggressive than what I had had to endure.

I was sure we had lost. The court broke for lunch, and I headed out to get some space and process what I had witnessed.

On our return, the judge summarised for the jury.

He talked at great length about all the charges made and what the prosecution must prove for them to be without any doubt. He explained how they had to look at all the evidence before coming to a decision.

He highlighted what had been said. The strengths and weaknesses of each side and once he had finished, he dismissed the court.

I went home, home to being Dad to my kids, back to my everyday life while I waited for their decision.

It took two days for that call to come from my DC, it was just after 3.30pm on a Friday afternoon. I had just gotten home from picking up our two kids from school with Kevin, my mobile phone rang as the kids rushed upstairs to get changed.

I walked out into the back garden and closed the patio doors behind me, my hand shook as I slid across the answer button on the screen. I readied myself for disappointment again.

"Hello?" a female voice came through

"Hi" I answered, my voice was a little too high pitched and joyful, as my body was overcompensating for the sickness that now raged through me.

"The jury has been back, and they have given their verdict". I tried to tell by the tone of the policewoman's voice what the news might be.

"Are you home alone?" she asked

I told her that Kevin was upstairs with the kids as we had just gotten home from the school run.

"OK, so, Sid, are you ready?"

My mouth started to dry up again, I looked up to the sky and sent out a quick silent prayer to God. Please let it be good news, I pleaded.

"He has been found guilty on nine of the ten charges."

The November sun shone down on my face, caressing me and amplifying the joy that ripped through all my senses. I stood there in silence, the child's voice inside me yelling "Yes, Yes, Yes!" I couldn't believe what I was hearing; I had been convinced that he would get away with it, that it would be another hung jury.

"Are you there? Hello?" the voice on the other end of my phone brought me back to reality.

I remember asking if she was sure? What did this mean? And made statements of how I couldn't believe it, how it was finally over, and again how I couldn't believe it. My eyes wept, and I kept laughing, unable to control my feelings.

She went on to tell me that he was found guilty of five accounts of indecent assault, two accounts of gross indecency and two accounts of buggery (Rape). The one charge that he hadn't been found guilty of was the sexual abuse he had put me through on a school holiday on a boating trip up the river Thames, where he had made me masturbate him and give him oral sex at night with only a curtain to divide us from the other boys as they slept.

It had happened, and the DC was quick to reassure me that she knew it was true. She went on to explain that the jury probably just couldn't get their heads around the thought that someone would take such a risk at being caught. Child abusers do, often, it must add to the thrill of it for them.

The DC checked that I was OK and told me to go and tell Kevin and enjoy the weekend.

I ended the call and stood staring down our garden. A tingle rushed through my body while my head just spun in sheer shock and joy.

I turned around to go into the house, Kevin was in the kitchen watching me through the patio doors, the children were still upstairs.

He asked me if it was the call I had been waiting for, I told him it was. He then asked me what the verdict was, I told him, and he hugged me close to his chest, and I cried. His arms held me tight, and he whispered to me that I was safe. My body shook as I cried, Kevin's chest also shook as he cried too.

My body let go of all the anxiety, worry and stress and the tears just flowed. My head raced with thoughts. I couldn't believe that after decades of people not believing me, I was finally being heard. I remembered how my social worker had done nothing to help me when I was a boy. How the last trial had been a hung jury, but that justice was finally served. At last people, society, and the law was saying sorry to me and recognising the horror that I had endured and that had plagued my life for so long after.

The kids came downstairs and saw us crying, and their little faces went grey with worry, so I knelt down and spoke to them.

Because the investigation and the two trials had gone on for so long, I had told them both previously that I was going to court because a man from my childhood had been very nasty to me. I had kept it simple, and I had, of course, left out the sexual abuse.

Now I could tell them that he had been found guilty, that 12 people had believed me and that he would soon be going to prison. My daughter, just ten years old at the time walked over to me and just hugged me. It was the perfect ending.

CHAPTER NINE

People have different views on what should happen next, how I should be feeling and of course what I should do with my new life.

Many times, I've heard people, with good intentions, tell me how great it must be to be able to move on and let go of the past. But the truth is that for me, I can't, not entirely anyway.

It's been over 18 months since the rapist was sentenced to 15 years, he will serve half of that and be on license for the rest of his life. He is now a registered Child Sex Offender.

His wife has divorced him, and their family home and the life they had for so long together is all gone.

He has lost a son, and a son has lost his father, and from whichever angle you look at it, that is not something to be celebrated.

A family has learnt that their son, brother, cousin and uncle was not who they believed him to be, that he is a monster, a being that preys on the weak, the forgotten, and those that are unable to stand up for themselves.

I hope that the man who had also been preyed on for years by Andy before I had joined the school can now find peace. He had been interviewed by the police as part of the investigation and had corroborated everything I had said, but he couldn't face giving evidence in court as it would mean having to tell his wife and kids about something he had kept hidden for so long. I understand that, and I hold no malice against him.

I hope that anyone that is vulnerable that came across him in his role of social worker, who he may have raped or abused, now knows that he is gone. I am proud of myself for removing him from society so that others are safe, but I am also tinged with a little guilt because it would have been better if I had done it years ago.

I have been told that he continues to show no remorse or acceptance and won't attend any therapy, but I can't dwell on that, that next chapter is for him to write.

For me, much has changed and yet much stays the same. I am still the boy that was raped, and I am still the boy that wasn't listened to, that was ignored when I told others about what was happening. I still live with a crippling depression that few understand and an anxiety that occasionally keeps me locked in at home. I am still on my antidepressants, but now I am comfortable with that and probably will be on them until my last day on earth.

I am still the man that use to cut himself on his arm when he was in this early 20's to relieve some pain, and I am still the man that became terrified after leaving school that his homosexuality was a by-product of being raped and abused. I dated many girls and had a lot of heterosexual sex that I didn't enjoy, to "cure" myself while causing some adorable young women a lot of heartache.

The young man that drank too much and took too many pills, who ended up homeless on the streets of Brighton, sleeping underneath the pier with all the drunks for a year, and who prostituted himself in public toilets to survive still lives within me. As does the guy who couldn't take any more pain in his life and walked to the local train station and sat on the platform in the heavy winter snow waiting for a train to come so he could end it all. They are all still here, all apart of who I am, but now, I am also the boy that survived, that got justice, that took control and took their life back. I can give the boy that I was, the nurturing and love that he deserved. I am strong enough to protect him now, and I proudly talk of him and share his story of courage.

But I am uncertain about who I am now, my life is in HD and as corny as it sounds, I see the beauty in what is all around me now. I see the world differently, I look at the opportunities that I was blind to for so many decades. I see love, I feel love, and I am able to love, without being on guard. Yes, it is still easier for me to give love than receive it but I'm getting there.

I am now in my late 40's, yet I am learning new things about myself. I react differently, I've been told I smile and laugh more, I'm less defensive, more tactile.

I am a better person for seeking justice and opening up about what happened.

For decades, I was fuelled by a need to protect myself, keep everyone at arm's length. I had never liked myself.

I was the boy that no one listened to, the boy whose parents put him into care and never came back. The boy who was treated as if he didn't matter, the boy that told himself throughout all the abuse and neglect that "It didn't matter, it's only me."

I took that all in and it grew inside my tiny body, it rewired me, and it told me every day that I didn't matter.

I have never expected to be successful nor have I expected too much from myself, and now I understand why. I am still plagued with self-doubt but now when I achieve something, each time I have a day free from anxiety and flashbacks, that hardwired self-loathing part of me crumbles away.

I am rediscovering things that I enjoyed before the abuse, like writing, singing, and art.

I still have days when I feel afraid and vulnerable. Nights when I can't sleep, dreams of what happened back at the school invade my head, visions of him attacking my kids, thoughts of him tracking us down when he is out of prison and destroying my family.

My life is full of triggers, a smell, a song from the 1980's, his name, a man with a similar build, seeing a van the same as the one he drove, all these things can and do send me back to being 11 years old. I can be a man and a child at any time throughout the day, memory and fear control my emotions and I often wonder who I would have become if I hadn't been violated.

Hearing the Judge sentence, him to 15 years in December 2015 didn't result in an end, not for me at least. I wish I could honestly say that it did, oh how I want that to be true! It was a powerful moment to hear the Judge state that what he had subjected me to was pure horror, evil and abhorrent. That he was a calculating man, who preyed on the small rejected boy that I was back then.

I was moved to tears when the Judge addressed me and praised me for my courage throughout both trials and his wish for me to be able to enjoy my family life and create new healthy memories. I looked over at Kevin, who was sat to my right and saw the tears roll down the side of his face as he squeezed my hand, confirming to me that he too was proud.

But to be honest, the investigation and the two trials had caused me to feel vulnerable again, because every raw emotion of fear and every memory of the physical pain had been refreshed inside me.

I could smell him, hear him, see him, and I could taste him ramming himself into my child mouth. The dryness of his cock and the sickening taste of his excitement. Even, over a year on, I can be sent back into that shower or his bedroom or my bunk bed in the blink of an eye.

I truly dislike the term Historical Sexual Abuse because it's not historical when you must revisit it in great detail. When you are questioned and doubted it brings it all back, every bit of fear and pain is real again. It doesn't diminish; you just learn to lock it down deep inside.

It seems to me the only thing I can do about this is live with it, be honest about it and share it with those that understand it and do something positive with it.

I often worry that Kevin will get bored or exhausted by that side of me that is still vulnerable, so I hide it as best as I can. I don't always tell him when I've had a day where I have been fearful or plagued by memories, and he won't be happy to read that.

I don't want him to be my carer, he is my husband, my lover and my best friend and that is how it must stay.

When the kids are around its easy for me to ignore the negative, I go into Dad mode and then there is no room for anything else other than my kids and their needs.

I have had some counselling, and to a degree, it has worked. I have been able to get answers from myself by talking to someone, expressing the feelings and thoughts have led me to provide the solutions that I needed. But I gave it up as the anxiety of knowing I had counselling coming up in a day or two was too much for me and would make me unwell.

I have recently started up a local social/support group for men who have survived childhood abuse and rape. It is a place to meet, to share with people that understand the down times and fears. It's a place to grow and heal together and form friendships.

It is based in Brighton & Hove and is called ROAR – Reaching Out After Rape.

There are some great organisations out there for people who have survived childhood abuse and rape, that offer individual and group therapy as well as helplines and online chat. I would wholeheartedly recommend them all to anyone in a similar position. A list of them can be found at the back of this book.

CHAPTER TEN

The hard, horrible truth is that there are thousands of children that are currently living in fear, that are being raped, abused and groomed every day in our country and millions throughout the world and that is just not acceptable. Hundreds of adults are still living with the damage and fear from the abuse that they have also endured, too afraid to come forward, worried that they will not be believed, not supported and not taken seriously.

So many people, like myself, have lived years with the belief that they don't matter, so therefore what is happening to them doesn't matter too, but of course, that is wrong. It takes, on average, 26 years for a man to come forward and talk about the rape and abuse he has endured. That's 26 years of self-loathing, or low self-esteem and usually, of self-medication.

It is up to every single one of us to change society, to change how we react to child abuse and rape. We need to stop making jokes about sexual violence, and we need to stop turning a blind eye to our children's relationships with others. Take notice people! Meet who they are seeing! For their sake listen to your child, be aware of them. Talk to them, be honest about the dangers and make sure they know that no one has the right to touch them sexually without their permission and NEVER as a child. Make sure they know they can turn to you and talk to you at any time of the day or night.

One of my most significant hang-ups is that I hate not to be listened to. Even now it infuriates and hurts me when I am trying to get something across, and I am not being heard, or I am being spoken over. That I know stems from my time in care and at the boarding school.

If one person had stopped to give me time to talk about what was happening it could have ended what was happening to me as a child! if my social worker and headmaster had taken what I had said to them seriously and acted on it, it could have been stopped. If my foster family had stopped to wonder why my behaviour in the school holidays was so erratic, rather than just labelling me as a difficult child, it could have been prevented.

Notice your children, ask yourself why has their behaviour changed so much. Get off your android phone or iPhone or tablet, turn off the TV and get to know your child. It is literally that easy to notice a change in behaviour or their appearance when you are paying attention.

I am lucky, I have had justice, society and the law have recognised that what I lived through was sickening and damaging, but there are far too many cases of child abuse and rape going unnoticed. I believe that for each brave soul that comes forward and tells their story, for each celebrity that goes public with their story, for each guilty verdict, for each time a police officer shows a victim that they are believed, that we are making it a safer world for our kids. We have to make it harder for these predators to satisfy their needs. Us survivors have to shine our light, shine it brightly so we can stop these monsters from hiding in the darkness.

Justice doesn't remove the memories but what it does, is give the survivor strength and validity. Each time a person says I believe you and I am sorry you went through that; a soul is repaired a little bit more.

For years I didn't want to be known as the boy who was raped and abused. I didn't want the pity; the sympathy was too late by then. However, after the trial, after the support, after the justice, I have seen that what I went through is an integral part of who I am today, and I am not ashamed of it.

I am proud that I am a survivor and it makes me a better person, a better husband, and a better parent. As I said earlier in the book I am learning who I am every day, I respond differently to people and my environment, I am kinder to myself, and I forgive people for hurting me.

I have said my apologies to the people I have hurt. and without making excuses, I am able to give a reason to it.

Some people don't like the new me, the real me, the person I should have always been, and that's Okay. Some people thrived on my anger and insecurities and used it for their gain, and that can't happen anymore.

For those that have forgiven me and tried to understand, I am very grateful, for those that can't or won't, that's fine too, and I wish you all the best.

For anyone that may read my story and has had similar experiences, please speak up, you deserve so much better. You are so much better than what happened to you.

Even if there can be no legal justice for you, there can be healing, love, and friendship from others.

Seek support, go to the Dr or contact a support service. I can't put in words how strong and powerful you will feel, as well as proud of yourself for taking that first step.

Since December 2015, I have been asked if I forgive my abuser. It's a question that I have answered in many different ways over the months that followed.

Over time, after seeking support from some incredible groups, after talking openly and after writing this book. I can honestly say that I do forgive him.

I must; because if I don't, I won't sleep, I won't be able to enjoy the good memories, make new memories, enjoy my family or like who I am. I wouldn't be able to forgive my mother or my father or all the foster families and social workers that let me down so badly. Everything will be tainted with what had happened; as it has been for decades, I would continue to live in fear and in the past, and I just can't do that anymore.

So yes, I do, I forgive him because I want to live, I want to be happy, and I want to help others, and more importantly I want to help my children heal from their pasts.

My forgiveness doesn't make what he did any less horrific, it doesn't stop the memories or indeed the anger I feel, but it helps me to live the life I deserve.

I believe that rape and abuse aren't just about taking from the body, it is so much more than that. It destroys the very soul of the victim, it dislodges their core, and without help, it just won't heal.

The physical side heals fast, but the spirit, the emotions, the soul slowly dies once it has been invaded. Every survivor needs help to recover.

Every person is damaged and needs someone to say that they see that in them, and they are sorry for what they went through. The self-worth needs to be re-ignited, and that can happen through friendship, love, and someone to share it with.

Not every survivor can receive justice through the law, some of us are lucky enough for that to happen but it sadly isn't the case for everyone.

Some attackers can't be found, or a survivor might just not be brave enough to come forward, or too much time might have lapsed, and the pervert may have died.

During the investigation, I learnt that a couple of years before I came forward to the police that another old pupil from the same school had come forward, disclosing that he too had been raped, this time by the headmaster, Gerald, for some years. Unfortunately, when the police went to interview him, the headmaster had passed away. Over the years I was there, I knew of 12 boys that had been systematically raped and abused.

There are many ways for a survivor of rape and abuse to heal and regain control, and a big part of that is through the help of their family, friends, community and local services.

I said it before, I believe that each time someone comes forward, each time another story of justice hits the news, another conviction is successful, another police officer tells someone who has come forward that they believe them, that another one of us tells our story, it helps to give the hidden survivors a voice and the strength to go ahead.

We are making it a safer world for our young because we are educating them to talk about it and we are making it more difficult for these vile creatures to prey on our kids.

Chapter Eleven

The 1990's

In the early 1990's, life in Brighton began to improve for me. I had been lucky enough to get help from a friend and his family, which meant I was off the streets and could stop prostituting myself to survive.

They had kindly taken me in for a few months and had welcomed me into the family life. They had shown me what I had been missing for so many years, the friendship and love of a family unit. I began to relax and enjoy myself. I managed to eventually, get a small bedsit in the Seven Dials area of Brighton, where I had in fact been born in 1969, and I had a job, working as a sales advisor at The Body Shop. My relationship with my sister was growing as we began to spend time together.

I used to go clubbing and to the bars with a couple of friends of mine, and I was happy. At one of the bars I met a hairdresser called Calvin, he was older than me, by about 20 years, if my memory serves me right, and he had a small salon in the North Laines area of town.

He was a fashion conscious, sociable person, with his dark hair and green eyes, he was very handsome, and he knew it. I was in my early 20's, with my bleached Bros hair, ripped faded jeans and bomber jacket, music, fashion and socialising were all that was important to me.

I drank daily, I partied every weekend, and I took recreational drugs, such as speed and cocaine.

One evening, after I had finished work and had been home to get washed and changed, I arrived at Calvin's flat at around 7 pm. There was a group of guys there, about 5 or 6, all in the 30's and 40's, as well as two guys around my age that I knew from the clubs. They were all drinking and enjoying themselves, and it was evident that Calvin was very high on drugs. Music blared throughout the one bedroomed flat.

He offered me a choice of cocaine or ketamine, but I refused as I was tired and had hoped for a quiet evening. He teased me and told everyone how miserable I was being, and they all cheered and laughed, raising a glass to their intoxicated host.

I went into the bathroom to see if there were any headache tablets and while I was in there, Calvin came in behind me. He handed me a glass of white wine and kissed me on the lips, as he left the room he told me to wash the headache tablets down with the wine and join the party.

I took the tablets and went into the lounge; the music was pumping and mixed in with the laughter and cheering of the other guys, I knocked back the rest of the wine and poured myself more.

I wasn't going to be able to have my quiet night in, so I decided I'd better join in.

I opened my eyes, and my head throbbed with pain. It was worse than the headache from earlier, and I felt disorientated and sick. I sat up and tried to focus my sight as it was blurry, as my eyes began to tune themselves in I realised I was on Calvin's bed, in his bedroom, alone and that my trousers weren't on.

As I lay my head back down on the pillow, trying to work out why I was in the bedroom, the door creaked open, and Calvin walked in.

He seemed calmer and soberer than the last time I had seen him and asked me how I was.

I told him how unwell I felt and asked him why I was on the bed; he went on to say to me that my headache hadn't cleared, and he had told me to sleep it off.

"What time is it?" I asked.

He looked at his watch and told me it was 9.45 in the evening. Was I confused? It had only been 7 pm when I had arrived, where had the time gone.

He offered to get me some fresh water and left the room momentarily.

I sat up and tried to get my thoughts together and then it hit me, memories of men's face's peering in close to me, laughter, the smell of wine on their breaths, memories of being touched, images of several erect cocks surrounding me.

Calvin walked in, and I told him what I was remembering, he said to me it must have been a dream and handed me the glass of water, I took a mouthful but spilled some. I looked down at where the water had gone on the bed and saw a bottle of poppers lying next to me, and I also noticed that my t-shirt was stained and stuck to my stomach.

I pulled up my top and noticed my skin was dry and flaky, the material of the t-shirt was stiff in some areas. I realised it was dried sperm.

I looked up at Calvin, he smiled at me, it wasn't a friendly smile but more of a sympathetic smile, pity was written across his face or was that an apology.

As if suddenly having a super speed memory download, my head was full of images and sounds.

Faces, men, laughter, poppers being passed around and rammed under my nose, sweating faces, cocks being masturbated and visions of various heads going down on me.

I then, at that moment, realised what I was seeing. I had been sexually abused again, but how? I must have been drugged.

I looked at Calvin.

"The wine, you bastard, you drugged my wine!" Calvin approached me, he sat on the bed and went to touch my head.

I recoiled back, jumped off the side of the bed, I grabbed my trousers that were on the floor next to my trainers, and I ran out of the flat. Once in the communal hallway, I got dressed and left the building.

I walked home to my bedsit, numb with shock, numb but in pain inside, my body was screaming with anger.

My head was full of one thing only, my voice, and it was telling me.

"It's doesn't matter; it's only you."

Chapter Twelve

The Letter

Andy,

It's been two years now, since you were found guilty of the systemic abuse and rape of me as a child all those years ago.

It has been a period of healing for me, as well as a time to visit the terrifying memories and relive the physical pain that you put me through as a young child for so many years. A time to let go of the horror and to be who I always should have been.

The damage to my soul has had an enormous impact on my life, and I feel strongly that you should hear about it.

When someone, like you, rape's a person, a child, forcing them to experience an invasion that is not only physical but also emotional, you shatter them into a thousand pieces. The very person they were before you touched them is destroyed, tainted and never the same.

Physically, you tore at my inner flesh, causing me to bleed, creating a wound, that to this day, still hasn't healed. Emotionally you taught me that the only way for me to matter was for me to give every part of me over. For my small child body to be used and violated, in ways that my innocence had never been aware was possible and that pain has followed me into much of my adult life.

You confused my mind, on the one hand, you were my friend, my big adult friend who treated me to sweets, cans of fizzy drinks and any loose change that I could find in your work van. It is true that being your "boy," as I was known by teachers and pupils at the boarding school, gave me protection from the bullying from the other boys.

But when alone with you, after you had come and collected me from my bed or instructed me earlier that day to go to your room, you did things that were worse than what any of the other kids could have done, you hurt me, controlled me, forced me and raped me.

I hadn't realised until I had to face you in court how angry, how inverted and how defensive I had been living my life since. The bile of fear and pain that swelled inside me was a blunt reminder of the harm you had done. It also brought with it a realisation of how I had used all that anger I had towards you against so many that came into my life over the years. A deeply wired mistrust of everyone.

However, what I also learnt through the two trials was how strong I am, how the boy that I was, still lived inside me and was using my physical strength to fight back and to ROAR.

Despite the damage you did to me you also gave me strength, strength to survive and thrive, to break the vicious circle of low self-esteem that you had rammed into me.

You deserve to be where you are now, not only because of what you did to me but also because of what you did to the boys before me and to any others that possibly came afterward.

I doubt very much that I was the last, that I was the one who satisfied your sick cravings.

You deserve to be where you are because you have taken no responsibility or shown any remorse for your actions. Your actions have destroyed your own family, the lies that you have told, the secret life you have led, have all been brought out into the light.

I hear other survivors of rape and violence say how they don't hate their attacker, and I understand that. It isn't with kindness towards you that I say that, it's just that you are insignificant to me. I don't wish any harm to come to you because I am, and always have been, a better person than you. But it was important that you were held accountable for what you did. I hope you will use the time you have inside to work on yourself, to heal, to learn and to realise what you have done but somehow, I doubt you will.

The world we live in is changing fast, and the forgotten, the voiceless, the attacked, the survivors and the minorities are fighting back. Beasts like you are being and will continue to be held accountable and punished for the harm that you all do.

Don't sit in your prison cell feeling angry or seeking revenge, because you can't hurt me or anyone else again, think about how you can right the wrongs, how you can be a better person, how you can heal.

I am not afraid of you anymore, and you have no hold over my life.

Sid Spencer

Useful Services:

Survivors UK: Offering individual counselling, group work, and a helpline service. Based in London but covering the whole of the UK. www.survivorsuk.org

Mankind: Based in Sussex. Providing confidential services to men who have been affected by unwanted sexual experiences. www.mankindcounselling.org.uk

Life Centre: Based in West Sussex. Offering a national helpline and a counselling team in Sussex for survivors of rape and sexual abuse. https://www.lifecentre.uk.com

The Survivors Trust: Providing support, advice, and information on services across the UK. www.thesurvivorstrust.org

The Samaritans: Offering a safe place to talk, at any time you like. www.samaritans.org

Stay Brave: Signposting to appropriate services for help. Campaigning and developing policy so that all survivors can access the services they need. www.staybrave.org.uk

ROAR: Reaching Out After Rape: A Sussex based group. We offer socialising and friendship with other men who have been raped or abused as a child. Signposting to other services. www.roarbrighton.co.uk

Printed in Poland
by Amazon Fulfillment
Poland Sp. z o.o., Wrocław